marketing
stripped bare

marketing
stripped bare

AN INSIDER'S GUIDE TO
THE SECRET RULES

PATRICK FORSYTH

**KOGAN
PAGE**

London and Sterling, VA

First published in Great Britain entitled *Everything You Need to Know About Marketing* in 1990
Revised edition 1995
Second edition 1999
First published in Great Britain and the United States entitled *Marketing Stripped Bare* in 2003 by Kogan Page Limited

120 Pentonville Road
London N1 9JN
UK
www.kogan-page.co.uk

22883 Quicksilver Drive
Sterling VA 20166-2012
USA

© Patrick Forsyth, 1990, 1995, 1999, 2003

ISBN 0 7494 3997 1

British Library Cataloguing-in-Publication Data

A CIP record for this book is available from the British Library.

Library of Congress Cataloging-in-Publication Data

Forsyth, Patrick.
  Marketing stripped bare / Patrick Forsyth.
    p. cm.
"First published in Great Britain entitled: 'Everything you need to know about marketing' in 1990."
Includes bibliographical references and index.
    ISBN 0–7494-3997-1 (Pbk.)
    1. Marketing. I. Forsyth, Patrick. Everything you need to know about marketing. 2003. II. Title.
  HF5415.F5667 2003
    658.8–dc21

                                                      2003002585

Typeset by JS Typesetting Ltd, Wellingborough, Northants
Printed and bound in Great Britain by Biddles Ltd, Guildford and King's Lynn
www.biddles.co.uk

Contents

Foreword

Marketing consists of the anticipation, identification and fulfilment of customers' needs. It is, or should be, at the heart of every commercial enterprise (and a good few non-profit organizations as well). The source of every organization's future cash flows is the customer, and it is the task of marketing to win customer preference. This requires highly professional marketers, but also a company-wide appreciation of the role and critical importance of marketing.

It suggests that many people around an organization – some would say everyone – can, indeed should, contribute in some way to marketing success. This gives rise to the concept of what is known as a *marketing culture*.

This Institute has always been unashamedly evangelical in its promotion of marketing, and has sought to convey something of the importance and excitement of marketing far and wide. Marketing people must be truly professional, and must remain so in a fast changing world. Others in many areas of business, some directly linked to marketing, others less obviously so, must understand – and often contribute – too.

This explanatory process of communication about marketing to a wider audience is a vital one, and any book that assists the process is to be commended. The novel approach Patrick Forsyth uses here makes this one accessible, and thus especially welcome.

John Stubbs
Chief Executive
The Chartered Institute of Marketing

Preface

Probably the best book on marketing ever written

Those involved in marketing believe it is, quite simply, the most important activity in business. Marketers are disarmingly modest. In addition, they believe marketing is the nicest thing you can do with your clothes on. Marketers are enthusiasts. What is more, they are right on both counts. So this is an important book.

Why exactly? Because marketing is probably the most confused and underestimated term in the business lexicon. Other areas of business may be complex, and you may not understand every detail of their workings, but you probably have a general sense of what they *do*. But marketing has, as we will see, a particularly wide canvas; marketing simply cannot be described the way in which we can say that production runs the factory and produces the product.

For many people marketing can stand some demystifying. Hence this book. So, if you want to understand marketing and marketing people better, you need to read this book. If you are just into marketing and struggling to get everything in perspective, or if you want to be in marketing, then again you need to read this book. Similarly, if you want to get the better of marketing people, or make use of marketing techniques in your private life – to advertise the old pram that has spent the last ten years in the attic, or persuade your bank manager to give you a loan – then you also need to read it.

Whatever your interest or involvement in marketing this is the book for you. So too if you are in functions of business other than marketing, or which constitute just a part of the whole process. At best it will make you rich, famous, successful in love and will cure warts. So buy it, now. It is not expensive for goodness sake, you need it, so stop cluttering up the shop just flicking through the pages and go straight to the cashier. Buy it, read it, and persuade your friends to buy it too; it could change all your lives. Better still buy two, then you will be twice as likely to find out what marketing is all about and the publishers might get rich even if you do not.

> Overheard
>
> A marketing man, tired of his job, gave it up and joined the police force. Some time later a friend asked how he was getting on. 'Well' he replied 'the pay and hours are not so good, but what I like best is that the customer is always wrong!'

Acknowledgements

When a manuscript is complete it makes you think. How did you ever persuade a publisher to turn your deathless prose into a book? And, having done so, how did you ever manage to get enough words down on paper in the right order and delivered on time? How many copies will it sell, and what will you spend the royalties on? Though, for most, substantial fantasies about the financial rewards of authorship are a bit like believing that you will win the lottery in time to pay off your credit card. You also realize that, despite your personal hard work and ego, it was not a solo effort.

So, in this case, thanks are owed. First to my various contacts at Kogan Page; this is not a typical book on marketing and I particularly wanted to execute it in the chosen style so as to make it accessible to a wide range of people – thank you for listening. Also to many people I have worked with or crossed paths with during my time in marketing consultancy and training. I have learnt much from many and been inspired by a few.

Particular thanks also to John Stubbs, Chief Executive of the Chartered Institute of Marketing, for writing the Foreword. Seemingly he shares my enthusiasm for spreading the word about the importance and excitement of marketing; as well he might considering his position!

Jo Owen prompted the title. Titles are not copyright and his book, *Management Stripped Bare* (which is to be recommended), is not about marketing, but thanks anyway.

Finally a necessary thank you to my bank manager. If there ever are any royalties, you will be the first to know (trust me).

Patrick Forsyth
Touchstone Training & Consultancy
28 Saltcote Maltings
Maldon
Essex CM9 4QP
United Kingdom

About the author

Patrick Forsyth is a marketing consultant and trainer of some years' experience; well, all right, more than 20 years' experience. He runs Touchstone Training and Consultancy which specializes in work in marketing, sales and communication skills.

He began his career in a major publishing group, where, having failed to become an editor (becoming an author is in the nature of revenge), he worked in sales, publicity and marketing before moving to a professional management institute and then into consultancy.

His training work includes public courses for commercial companies, management institutes and other professional bodies and tailored in-company courses for clients throughout a range of industries. He has worked in the UK, continental Europe and further afield, for example, in countries around South East Asia.

He is the author of a number of successful business books including *Marketing Professional Services, 101 Ways to Increase Your Sales* and *Writing Powerful Reports and Proposals* (all published by Kogan Page), as well as others on subjects ranging from career development and motivation to time management. In addition, he has edited books, advised on and appeared in a BBC programme on marketing and writes articles which have appeared in a variety of management magazines.

In fact, he writes and lectures on marketing at the drop of a hat; or for money. He is an enthusiast for his chosen field and hopes this particular book, which is designed to be particularly accessible, will act to cast a little light, demystifying marketing which is, after all, a vital component of the world of business.

> Some day I hope to write a book where the royalties will pay for the copies I give away.
>
> Clarence Darrow

1

Marketing in context

No customer can be worse than no customer

What is marketing? Well, for a start, it is sadly misunderstood by many, including some who work in it. So let us start by describing not what it is, but what it is not. Marketing is not a euphemism for advertising. Nor for selling; though both are important elements of marketing.

It is in fact much more than this, but the word confuses because it is used in at least three ways.

Marketing defined

First, marketing is, or should be, a philosophy of business. That of seeing the business through the eyes of the customers and ensuring profitability by providing them with value satisfaction. The reverse of saying 'This is what we make, buy some', it ensures the business focuses on customer needs.

Second, marketing is a function of business, the total management function that co-ordinates all that the philosophy implies, anticipating the demands of customers, identifying and satisfying their needs by providing the right product or service at the right price, time and place.

Third, marketing is an umbrella term for a series of techniques which are used to carry out the whole process. These include advertising and selling, plus a plethora of other promotional techniques and everything from research to pricing.

Together these three certainly show at once some of the complexity of marketing. The first implies that everyone in the business is involved, that everyone has to adopt the right attitude and many have specific roles to play. The second implies that someone has to wear the 'marketing hat', and do so at a sufficiently senior level to drive the whole process. The third shows the breadth of techniques necessary for the marketer and his team to ply their trade. No wonder marketing people believe they are important.

If all this seems a touch complicated just to get the goods to market, perhaps so, but it is necessary. This was not always the case. Originally marketing did not exist.

When the more entrepreneurial Neanderthals were trading axe-heads – 'three for the price of two, and I'll throw in a spare handle' – in exchange for, say, a week's supply of mammoth pie, there was little choice. Mammoth pie might not be the gastronomic treat of the millennium, but deep pan pizza was in short supply so if you wanted axe heads – no choice. Some years later and things were still very much the same: when Henry Ford began to mass-produce his cars you could have any colour you liked as long as it was black. And they sold in thousands.

Then after the second world war, as industry restarted, choice began to proliferate. Suddenly there were many kinds, shapes and colours of everything. Just deciding what to make and hoping people would come running for it was no longer enough. Customers now had choice. Whatever an organization supplied, and however good they thought it was, there was now the distinct possibility of customers finding something they liked more; and voting with their feet. And increasingly, they did. So marketing was invented. A revolutionary new business philosophy that looked at business through the eyes of the customers. Clever that, no wonder it took the Americans to think of it. Anyway it spread throughout the commercial world spawning a plethora of techniques designed to ensure customers' needs were met and that the said customers parted with their money promptly and repeatedly.

Marketing advocated a more professional, more scientific approach to the whole commercial process. Now its approaches are applied, with varying degrees of success and sophistication, by a wide range of organizations. By manufacturers of everything from frozen peas to word processors, and from bicycles to jet fighters. By providers of services from hoteliers to accountants. And by charities, environmental groups, even governments. The range of new or improved techniques that were now needed to keep ahead, even to keep up in the new more competitive business world, produced a new breed of senior managers able to co-ordinate the whole function and others to work with the individual techniques.

Marketing: art or science?

But the techniques of promotion, advertising and selling are not precise in their effect. They, and marketing itself, are as much art as science. So the good marketers are as creative as they are technically able; whether they succeed or not may have as much to do with experience, and with 'gut-feel' as it does with following the rules. They are the modern-day commercial alchemists; except that instead of eye of toad and wing of bat their ingredients are USPs, copy platforms, self-liquidating offers and brand strategies. Perhaps more than any other management function marketing thrives on jargon; and whilst jargon is only professional slang, it is invaluable in an activity where the great thing is to appear more scientific than artistic.

Qualifications and competencies

There are no standard qualifications for marketing. Well there are, but they in no way guarantee to equip those so qualified with anything but the qualification. Marketing is a practical art; all that matters ultimately is results and profits. Whilst there are, of course, well qualified marketers, there are also those who emerge from business school with the diplomas, but who have no commercial sense, or management ability whatsoever. This does not stop them having an inflated idea of their own value; indeed one marketing wag insisted he had found the perfect new business venture 'buying MBAs for what they are worth and selling them for what they think they are worth'. One suspects that this idea has not got off the ground only because the large number of MBAs working in those organizations providing venture capital do not themselves agree.

So, while qualifications can be useful, other things are essential. Certainly the successful marketer needs knowledge of the major marketing methods and techniques; and while he must, if he aspires to top management, be a jack of all trades, he must also be the master of some. In every industry the marketer must be able to communicate effectively and persuasively with customers. He must be effective at managing people, able to get things done through the team he manages. Like all managers, he will find this is not just a matter of telling people what to do. They must be directed, but also led, inspired, given a challenge, and given their head. The marketing team is crucial, the marketer must recruit the right people, then support them so that they do the job he wants. You cannot hire Einstein, then turn down his requisition for a blackboard.

Marketers must operate both tactically, being quick on their feet, and strategically, taking the long view and acting as puppet master. They must be numerate; increasingly so, as the need for analysis and quantification of everything grows to such proportions that it is said that if you ask a marketing man how his wife is, he will answer 'compared to what?'

Additionally these days, marketers also need to have a degree of computer literacy. Computers, indeed all things IT (information technology), play an ever-increasing role in many aspects of the marketing process: this may encompass many things, from modelling markets to tracking customer behaviour in supermarkets through their use of smart cards.

Attitude and flexibility are just as important. The marketer has a broad remit within his company, he must understand and work with the other functions of the business – even to the point of trying to get on with the accountant! He must be forward looking and open-minded, recognizing the constantly changing markets in which he works and reacting accordingly. Above all he must be creative. If marketing is about anything it is about creating a difference. This is important at every level, a whole new approach to advertising the product or an apparently tiny difference to product specification. Either can frighten competitors and win over customers. However, one such idea is not sufficient. The marketer must continuously come up with new approaches if he is to keep ahead of competitors ever intent on leapfrogging.

Not surprisingly not all managers possess all these characteristics, particularly in balanced combination. None of these characteristics can be taken for granted. You might think everyone is in favour of change, at least where it promotes improvement. Change is a good thing. If you believe that, try walking into your office and saying 'Right, as of today there will be some changes round here'; just see what reaction you get. Yet marketing must be a force for change.

Above all, it and the people in it, must produce results. Marketers cannot rely on pomposity, pinstriped voices or position. They must be practical, able to make things happen both themselves and through their team, and be prepared to be judged by results. The marketing kitchen can be an especially hot one.

Do not despair however if you are not, yet, a marketing director or do not at present possess all the necessary characteristics to become one. With a degree of confidence a little knowledge can go a long way, and this book certainly contains a little knowledge. Put yourself in the position of the marketer for a while, and read on.

> Benjamin Franklin may have discovered electricity but it was the man who invented the meter who made the money.
>
> Earl Wilson

> I can honestly say mine is one of the few occupations where the less I do for my customers the more they like it.
>
> A dentist

Sex

It is said that the talented physicist, Professor Stephen Hawking, whose book *A Brief History of Time* topped the bestseller lists, was told by the publishers that every mathematical equation he included would reduce the book's sale proportionally. He risked just one, and his book was immensely successful.

Another publishing maxim is that any book with the heading 'sex' in its contents will sell more than one without. That apart it appears here to acknowledge the sexist nature of the text so far. Talk of marketers, marketing men, salesmen and others may be deeply insulting, so let's acknowledge that there are women in marketing and one or two that are even quite good at it. Actually, before the publishers (who employ rather a lot of women) are buried in letters of protest, let me acknowledge that there are many who are just as good as men and rather too many who are better. So until the English language comes up with a word that means 'he or she' you may take it that any such reference is intended to encompass both sexes.

> The appointment of a woman to office is an innovation for which the public is not prepared, nor am I.
>
> Thomas Jefferson

> Whatever women do, they must do twice as well as men to be thought half as good. Luckily, this is not difficult.
>
> Charlotte Whitton

A bridge over troubled water

Marketing acts as a bridge between an organization and the outside world, its markets and customers. Both sides of the bridge must be firm before it is safe to cross.

The company

Marketing may be important but there are actually other functions and disciplines in business. The two main ones are finance and production. The accountants and production people involved think they are pretty important too.

Although all three functions are concerned to contribute to the same end, a profitable company, they often form an uneasy alliance. Since each area attracts different people with different attitudes some conflict is inevitable. (Relax, your company is normal after all.) In some companies this is extreme; there are many a firm where the only thing on which the marketing manager and the production manager work together is how to get the better of the accountant.

Take time, for example. In each area of business time is viewed differently. In finance the accountant is concerned predominantly with the past; he is a sort of corporate scorekeeper. The production man is concerned with the present, keeping the factory moving; only the optimistic marketer is concerned with the future and customers' purchases to come. There are other differences too. The accountant and production manager are introspective, concerned with what goes on within the company, whilst the marketer looks outwards to the market. Money too is viewed very differently. It is well known that all accountants are mean, tightfisted and hate money being spent. When it is spent, it is gone. The marketers on the other hand see all spending whether on plant or promotion as an investment, a way of ensuring tomorrow's sales and revenue; they have a 'nothing ventured, nothing gained' attitude to money. Neither of them encourages the production man to get involved with money; he would only get the notes oily and drop the coins in the machinery making it grind to a halt.

Even the people themselves may be in contrast. The introverted, qualified, precise accountant and the more flamboyant marketer for example.

Whilst conflict and differences may be inevitable, the company that minimizes such internal frictions may well have an advantage. For most there are enough enemies amongst competitors without allowing civil war to break out.

The three functions of business are rather like a three-legged stool – just one weak leg and it falls over – and all are needed if the company is to be successful. In a real sense, however, marketing must lead. Profit is only earned from outside the company, from the market place. So unless marketing activity successfully produces customers who buy and come back for more, there is no revenue, no profit and nobody's wages or salary get paid.

Marketing culture

In a sense everyone is involved in marketing. And not just passively involved but actively doing something. In modern-day business everyone should be doing something. One person doing nothing is bad enough, and two people doing nothing, as one wag remarked, is too much work duplication. So from the highest to the lowest, everyone contributes to customer satisfaction and, therefore, to profit making. Or they should do. Real life is often very different.

You will know, whatever your involvement, or lack of it, in marketing, the frustrations of being a customer. If marketing starts with the customer, succeeds through providing customer satisfaction at a profit, why, you may ask, is it often so very difficult to buy things? You know the story – 'There is no demand for that' (when you are standing there asking for it); 'We've run out of that'; 'Of course I don't know how it works, I only sell it'; 'Delivery is 8 weeks', or 18 or 80. It is no different in the supermarket or shop, from how it is in industry. It is an attitude that occurs both at the time of purchase and afterwards. When did you last try to get something repaired or serviced? 'Who sold you this then?' says the repair man, shaking his head sadly. And you know not only that it will be difficult to fix but that it was a bad buy in the first place. Of course good service does exist, but frankly prevailing standards are often low. And that makes for an opportunity, any company that can get these elements right, will, provided it has a good product, tend to thrive.

This, in turn, means steps have to be taken to initiate involvement throughout the company. The successful organization needs what is called a *marketing culture*. Many a marketer would equate this with dragging their non-marketing colleagues kicking and screaming into the 21st century, though if it can be done it often creates a genuine edge in the market place.

The market

This is the battlefield where the marketing battle takes place. Customers, who make up the market, are volatile in their likes and loyalties, the market place is an unpredictable arena and there are competitors and restrictions at every turn like rocks in a stormy sea.

Consumer marketing

In consumer marketing, products or services are sold to individuals: toothpaste, beer, instant coffee, motor cars, take-away Chinese dinners, dry cleaning, carpets. The marketing of such products is more visible, often more reliant on the use of advertising and regarded by some as more glamorous. The much advertised, repeat purchase, products in this category are known as FMCGs, fast moving consumer goods (jargon used to good effect by the market-ing director of a company making ammunition who described himself as marketing 'the fastest moving consumer goods of all').

Industrial marketing

Industrial products may be less visible but the range of products is, if anything, even greater, from aircraft to computers to paper clips for the office, machines for the factory, and oil or spares to keep them running, all sold to buyers in commerce and industry.

Industrial marketing, which tends to be equated with the heavy end of commerce such as engineering, has been largely replaced with the term *business-to-business marketing*. This is self-explanatory and encompasses the sale of both products and services.

Derived demand

This dictates that the bottling plant does not buy bottles unless customers are buying the soft drinks or beer that goes into them from the supermarkets. The chain of events involved can be lengthy. The estate agent sells the manufacturer a factory, he buys machinery to go in it, raw materials to make, say, bottles, plus everything from labels to stick on them to soap for his workers' washroom. Ultimately he sells his bottles to a bottler, who is buying or making soft drinks to put in them; the bottler sells to a wholesaler, who sells to the corner shop who, finally, sells to Joe Public. After all that it seems a pity if the baby knocks it on the kitchen floor and it is wasted.

The term 'derived demand' describes this kind of relationship, the fact that sales of some things are dependent on the sales of other things.

Marketing methods

The principles of marketing are always similar, but clearly the methodologies employed in these different kinds of situation themselves vary. Each method (within a mix of methods) must be carefully chosen to suit what is being done overall. For instance, promotional coffee mornings may sell a lot of plastic kitchenware but they would be unlikely to sell many ball bearings even if off-duty works managers or production engineers could be persuaded to attend.

Market segmentation

Strictly speaking there is no such thing as 'the market' for anything. Markets are made up of *segments*. Marketers identify elements of their market as segments, groups of customers, with common and precise needs. Marketers set great store by these groups, indeed it has been said that there are two kinds of marketer, those who divide their markets into two and the rest. In fact they describe such segments in many ways, by geography, for example, or by customer type. Another term you will hear applied in a similar way is *niche*, or *market niche*. This is just a segment with an especially tight focus; alternatively it may mean that the marketer using the term is a touch pretentious and feels the word 'niche' is somehow superior to the word 'segment'.

Analysis of this sort allows products to be marketed very specifically to different groups of people. So you sell not just holidays for
retired people, but holidays for retired people wanting, and able to
afford, to see the world and with an interest in windsurfing or hang
gliding. The more accurately you can chart such groups the more
successfully you can direct marketing activity to them without
waste. There is no point in telling non-swimmers with three children
under five about octogenarian windsurfing holidays.

Segmentation describes a mid-point between the usually impossible
ideal of individual marketing and mass marketing. While people
within an identified segment are not identical in all their views and
needs, there are enough people with sufficiently similar needs to
allow this approach to work well.

You only have to look at the approach taken with commonly
advertised products to see the way segmentation is used. Consider
detergents. They are all there to wash clothes, but there are those
for people who want to get their clothes:

■ clean;

■ white (or even blue);

■ clean, white or blue cheaply;

or who want a product which while doing one of these things will
also:

■ soften the fabric;

■ avoid soaking;

■ work in cooler water;

and even, if possible, not make their hands bright red in the process.
But that is not all, next you have to choose between a powder and a
liquid and then . . . but you get the idea. When the first household
robots want their metal aprons washed in lubricating oil someone
will sell a detergent to do just that.

Rather as evolution produces life forms to colonize every available niche, so products appear to exploit every small market segment. Any company finding a segment that is not catered for, or poorly so, is on the way to marketing success.

In consumer markets market segmentation can be analysed very precisely using divisions called socio-economic groupings; these can be regarded simplistically as customers broken down by age and sex. What a way to go.

Despite Orwellian overtones, many a marketing plan is incomplete without the use of this marketing alphabet – A, B, C1, C2, D, E. This convenient short-hand way of referring to the peculiar British class-ridden society originated with social psychologists. At one time the terms related to what might be described as upper class, upper middle, middle, lower middle, working class and the poor. But things have changed dramatically and old certainties about class are dying fast. For marketing purposes, therefore, if for no other, the magic letters now refer to a complex correlation between social class and buying power. Indeed this system is rapidly being replaced by another with the unlikely name of ACORN. This will no doubt grow into something else in turn. In any case in recent years more popular, though less precise, descriptions have appeared. These include DINKIES (Dual Income, No Kids), DUMPIES (Desperately Under-financed Mortgage Paupers), WOOPIES (Well Off Older People) and SWELLS (Successful Women Earning Lots of 'Lolly'). There are even some versions for the marketers themselves such as the YARGGS (Young Aggressive Ruthless Go-Getters), a stage they grow out of all too quickly becoming SMARMS (Sophisticated Middle Aged Rejuvenated Marketers).

Some marketing activity is increasingly likely to be based on *demographic changes*. For example, in the UK the population is ageing and, at the same time, certain sections of older people have more disposable income than ever before. Because of this the market for retirement homes, cruises and income producing investments are all opportunity areas. Some changes have a detrimental effect on existing markets, others open up new opportunities. So, if no one had children until they were 35, this would affect the sale of a range of items from rusks to nappies, but those people would then have more money available to spend on, say, holidays. Successful marketers therefore watch for, and try to anticipate, any change that might affect their business and the needs it satisfies.

> Every crowd has a silver lining.
>
> P T Barnum

Competition and other difficulties

Marketing would be easy if you were able to do it in isolation. If your company was the only one marketing, let us say instant coffee, the world, or at least the coffee drinkers, would perhaps beat a path to your door. Needless to say nothing is that simple. There are a multitude of outside influences all conspiring to make things more difficult, whatever you market.

Competition is the most important. What exactly is competition? Well, surely, if you make, say, fountain pens then it is other fountain pen makers. But wait a minute, what else can you write with? Companies making pencils, ballpens, fibretip pens; all these are also your competition. And what about typewriters and word processors? Or dictating machines. It gets worse because some 80 per cent of all fountain pens are bought as presents, so you are in competition with everything from roller skates to book tokens; whatever a doting aunt may select as a suitable gift for a favourite spoilt nephew or niece.

Few, if any, businesses enjoy a monopoly, at least not for long (though why is there only one Monopolies Commission?). What is more, competition does not go about its business by carefully avoiding you. The car sticker which says 'Just because you're para-noid doesn't mean they are not out to get you' was obviously created for marketers. Competition *is* out to get you, and is everywhere, some even creeping up on you from overseas. Their marketing efforts are designed to sell their products *instead* of yours. *Every* organization has to worry about competition. Being big is no protection, it just means that there is more to lose.

> You can be a very big shark in your market place, but it's the piranhas that will take you apart.
>
> Sir Iain Valance

Marketing is warfare and competition deploys an ever changing armoury of weapons to secure an edge. You need to keep your eye on them, constantly. Better still, keep ahead of them, it is difficult to see the writing on the wall when you have your back to it.

More difficulties

As if it were not enough to contend with competition, there is a long list of other factors all apparently designed specifically to inhibit your marketing success. These include:

- *legal restrictions*, on practically everything from what you can say in your advertisements, to how you treat your employees. Kingsley Amis once proposed a model for the ideal advertisement 'Drink Amis beer – it makes you drunk'. Clear, informative and effective. But the Advertising Standards Authority insist all advertisements should be legal, decent and honest. So the idea has, sadly, never been used.

- *financial restrictions*, as there is never enough money to invest in marketing (at least lack of money is something you are probably used to at home). So this provides a brake on the process for most companies, but can give the larger firm with more resources an advantage. There are, of course, those resourceful Davids who rise to this challenge and even the large firm does well to remember Goliath.

- *labour restrictions*, as even in times of high unemployment many companies are held back because they cannot find the skilled people they need to make expansion possible. To demonstrate that skilled people are in short supply just think of the last time you needed a plumber in a hurry, or tried to recruit a new secretary.

- *foreign restrictions*, such as import duty at a level that prohibits your exporting to certain countries (it seems to be an unwritten rule that the more you want to visit a country the higher and more prohibitive its import duties on your product will be). There are those of course who are successful overseas, for instance two Arabs are discussing their recent visitor. 'What impressed you most about the Englishman?' one asks his friend who is holding a pair of skis. 'His salesmanship' he replies. Apparently no foreign restrictions there.

- *distributive restrictions*, for you may find difficulty with transportation, or with getting retailers, wholesalers, agents or distributors to stock your product.

- *demand restrictions*, and this is the ultimate one – if the market is not of sufficient size then you will never make a fortune. Marketing success means enough customers paying enough money for enough products or services to pay the bills and make a profit.

All in all the marketer lives a precarious and exposed existence. If you stick your neck out too far there is always someone, or something, that might cut it off. Stick it out not far enough and chances are lost, profits not made; finding the right balance is one of the skills of the marketer.

In addition, more recently, another has to be considered: *environmental restrictions*. The 'Green' movement shows, in microcosm, marketing at work. On the one hand greater awareness of pollution, and the health of everything from newts to whole rain forests as well as mere people, has had a restrictive effect. Government controls on pollution may put up production costs. This may make a product more expensive and more difficult to sell. Or it may create additional opportunities: when the car you buy *must* have a catalytic converter then customers must pay up – and the manufacturers of such devices can laugh all the way to the bank, and breathe more easily on the way.

At the same time customers have come to *want* green products. As a result it is now possible to buy a green just about anything. Green detergents may really do less harm to the rivers they end up in, other products may be labelled green because they are a little different from others, but still do no good to everything between the supermarket and the ozone layer. What is more, this area changes as you watch. Regulations proliferate and fashion plays a part too; so that every cause that hits the headlines means profit for someone. You need to watch the trends.

Spotting opportunities

As things in the world around us change, possibilities arise for marketing people to take advantage of. A sharp eye and a degree of prescience are necessary, but the rewards can be considerable.

> Opportunities are usually disguised as hard work, so most people do not recognize them.
>
> Ann Landers

An opportunity needs to be worked at and no idea is so good as to be guaranteed to lead to easy profits. First, however, opportunities must be spotted. Consider some examples of circumstances that may prompt this. Ecological changes have been mentioned as one factor creating opportunity. So too does legislation: legislation ending the supply of leaded petrol in the UK will help the sales of conversion kits, and of new cars, for example.

Social changes may be prompted by other influences in the way that more retired people with money to spend is a direct reflection of changing attitudes to work and savings, and of improved health care. Whatever the root cause, social and life-style changes are manna from heaven to the marketer. If they see that people are having babies later in life, they do not worry about the human race dying out, only about what they can sell such people in the interim. Then, if new parents are older, better established or better off, and less inclined to interrupt their careers with time off work – what does that imply? A bigger market for convenience items concerned with baby rearing and for crèches.

Every change is an opportunity for someone. Have you noticed that more people are under pressure at work? Fine, you can sell them a place on a seminar on 'Stress Management', aromatherapy, membership of a health club or a large gin and tonic on the way home. Whatever the pressurized may choose to do someone will be ready to take their money. Did you notice how people worried about the millennium bug? No matter that you and your computer colleagues caused the problem by forgetting that the year 2000 would come after 1999; sell them a disk to stick in the computer and sort it all out. Or, better still, a new computer. If you notice that some people will shop at two in the morning then you discover new retail opportunities. And have you noticed that more people are working from home? Excellent; think of all the equipment they will need to buy to make it possible.

What next? If the Government propose a tax on breathing, some alert marketer will be there to launch home oxygen tanks on the market or a measuring device to allow people to check whether their face is at a level of blue that demands they take their next breath. A major engine for change – and thus a major source of opportunities – is technology. With a computer in every home the market for games, or works of reference, on disk becomes obvious. More of this later.

Being able to anticipate change, and being ready with something that suits the new conditions – whatever they may be – is a valuable skill for anyone in marketing. Being able to do it accurately and well in advance is better. And if you can do it infallibly then you can name your price (but may need to make the most of it before you are burned at the stake).

> There's no difficulty so big or complicated that it can't be run away from.
>
> Graffiti

Creating the right mixture

Another important jargon term is the *marketing mix*, a description which encompasses the elements that are used by the marketer to bridge the gap between the company and the market. It is comprised of three separate elements:

- the *product* (or service) or product range;

- the *price*, and all the discounts and terms it includes;

- *presentation*, all the means of communicating with the market, including advertising, promotion and selling.

Like a cook, the marketer must juggle with the ingredients of his mix to create just the right mixture. Remember: all three elements of the mix are changeable, all have a different role to play for the marketer.

The product

Ideally you need a good one. Whatever your product it needs a *USP*. This is jargon for a Unique Selling Proposition ie a description of what makes your product different or, if it is in fact essentially the same as your competitors' products, a description that makes it seem different. Thus there are two types of USP:

1. *real USPs* – something about your product that makes it truly different from competitors. This might be the name, some bring this difference to a product by themselves like Rolls Royce or IBM. Or it will be a real factor about the product that creates the difference, the only washing up liquid with the added water softener.

2. *invented USPs* – qualities dreamed up about your product because it otherwise would not seem different. Sometimes these are the most effective: soap that puts you on the same footing as the film star; yoghurt that makes you fitter, slimmer and more attractive; toothpaste that will get you a partner across a crowded room.

The product on its own is not enough, it must have a product (or brand) *image*. This is what people *believe* about the product, it may differ from reality or have only a loose connection with the product. This association can be very strong; witness the quality image of Marks and Spencer. Create the right image for your product and the foundation for success is laid. Take the brand image too far and the name becomes synonymous not with the maker but with all products of the same kind. Thus we write a note in our 'filofax' with a 'biro' to go home and 'hoover' the living room.

Of course the name selected is important. If it is too much like another, then it may be illegal; passing off. If it is too bland no one will notice it; if it is too complicated then no one will be able to remember, pronounce or spell it. Having said that there are exceptions to every rule. For instance the name 'Smith' seems to help sell a great many crisps.

An alternative is to make up a name, indeed most brand names are just that. Even this is not as easy as it sounds. A multinational company may want a name that it can use, and its customers are happy with, in a dozen different markets. More than one product has failed because its name has turned out to have an unfortunate meaning in, say, Germany or Japan.

Looking overseas it seems unlikely that we will see products such as Bums Biscuits or Krapp toilet paper (Sweden), Dribly lemonade or Mukk yogurt (Italy), Bonka coffee (Spain), Pee Cola (Ghana), or Crapsy – a high fibre cereal – (France) launched in the UK without a change of name. Similarly, surely only the French could have named an after-shave Kevin; it may work for them, but I doubt it would ever become the height of sophistication in Britain. No one is immune from such dangers. Certainly if you look back you quickly come to a time when neither brand nor company names were chosen with the current need for taking such broad perspectives; or would respected corporate giant Fisons have picked a name that sounds identical to the Swedish word for fart?

Any trick may give the right effect, sticking with an original name but abbreviating it to initials for instance. There is something infinitely more classy about BMW than Bavarian Motor Works.

Another way is to give your product no name at all, but to sell it to someone who sells it under their name, as with the 'own brands' sold under the names of the big supermarket chains.

Image is important in any kind of marketing, and must be reflected in every aspect of operation, from the look of an office, the manner of the people, the name of the brand, the packaging, and the style of the promotion and advertising. It is the totality of all this that persuades.

> You can fool too many of the people too much of the time.
>
> James Thurber

Would that it was that easy. Ultimately a poor product cannot be carried by a positive image, and customers will not come back a second time if disappointed the first. Products must satisfy customers.

The non-product

A final point about products. There may not be one. It may be a service. The principles of *service marketing* are similar to product marketing but certain elements are different. Service marketing is particularly exposed and vulnerable. Reputations are hard won and easily lost.

In a hotel say, the vulnerability is clear, there are almost infinite opportunities for something to go wrong. And if 24 hour service refers to the length of time you have to wait for a sandwich, especially if you ordered eggs and bacon, then you tend to remember. What is more, informal research suggests that a dissatisfied customer will tell 10 times as many people as a satisfied one, enough to concentrate the minds of all service marketers. Dissatisfied customers not only do not return, they may also encourage others to do business elsewhere.

Bear in mind however that people buy neither products nor services, but buy *benefits*, that is what those products or services do for, or mean to, them. Hence the old expression – sell the sizzle not the steak. Or as the founder of a major cosmetics group put it, rather less kindly, describing the business thus 'In the factory we make cosmetics, in the market we sell hope!' In any case talking benefits is an important part of marketing; much that is said in advertisements, in promotional literature and by sales people should reflect this element of product or service description.

Setting the price

A major contributory factor to marketing success is getting the policy on pricing correct. Pricing is an area where elements of art and science are both essential, and where careful consideration can literally turn loss into profit. There is plenty of theory.

Take for instance the *elasticity of demand*, or indeed the reverse, the *inelasticity of demand*, concepts which address the question of whether if you put the price up you will sell less, or more, or the same, or not. It does not necessarily answer the question, but you can draw graphs of it and they always look splendid.

> People want economy, and they'll pay any price to get it.
>
> Lee Iacocca

What really matters is how much people see the product as worth, what they are in fact prepared to pay for it. Take *price plateaux*, the theory that prices over or under various round figures will affect the number sold. It is no accident that so much is priced at £4.95 or £9.99; customers really do feel it is less and are inclined to buy more. It really works: would you have bought this book for £15.00? Of course not. It also means the cashier has to open the till to give change and this reduces the incidence of fiddles at the checkout. (This is not unimportant, staff pilferage in retailers costs millions of pounds every year, which the customer, of course, ultimately pays.)

There are essentially three main approaches that can be adopted to setting a product's price:

1. The accountant's way or cost plus

This is calculated by working out what it costs to make the product, or supply the service, adding in an amount for overheads, distribution, advertising, etc then adding an appropriate percentage for profit. This should stop you making a loss, provided the sums are correctly calculated, but it can lead to inappropriate pricing because it is introspective, and takes no account of the market outside. Worse, no marketer wants a key decision like this reduced to a formula anyone else understands; least of all one that the accountant can calculate.

2. The pessimistic way

This means reviewing competition, seeing at what price other, similar, products are selling and setting your price low to avoid being undercut. Competitors must be taken into account but if their cost structure is different, and you follow it slavishly, you may even make a loss. If you are not very scientific about setting your price, maybe your competitors are not either and, before you know it, the blind are leading the blind.

3. The optimistic way

This looks at the market first, and asks what customers are prepared to pay. Often this will be more than the price arrived at by the other approaches. Customers will pay more for all sorts of reasons, quality, status, service and so on. Everyone knows brown eggs taste nicer than white, so why not ask a little more for them even though the insides are just the same?

Prices also have to reflect strategy. Thus a *skimming* policy sets a high price for a new product in the early stages of its promotion, to produce the maximum margin. This is seen in many areas of technological products, the first personal stereos were very expensive, but prices came down as more manufacturers entered the market. You can see the same thing happening today with many computer products. New ones cost more than a product that has been on the market for a while (this sometimes seems like about a fortnight). The opposite of this is *penetration* pricing, setting a low price to achieve the maximum number of sales and keep competition out.

Overall it often seems better to err towards a high price rather than a low one. You need the margin to finance your marketing activity, and you can always come down a bit if you get it wrong. Most successful products are not the cheapest amongst their competitors, just look at the leading brands in any supermarket to check. Customers may be emotive about price increases but in many cases they do not buy the cheapest, indeed they will equate quality, or status, with high price.

Lately another term has entered the marketing lexicon: *confusion pricing*. This describes situations currently the case for competing mobile phone networks and airline flights amongst others where the options facing the consumer are virtually unintelligible because of the multiplicity of overlapping options. Potential customers are encouraged to give up even trying to make any definitive comparison and select an option on some other basis.

> All right, so I like spending money! But name one other extravagance!
>
> Max Kauffmann

Not all prices are fixed. Often the price, terms, discounts vary with quantity bought, and the importance of the customer. Another stock in trade of the marketer is negotiating skill. These days many customers are as good at this as the salespeople who supply them. Negotiation can develop into either a subtle interplay of to-ing and fro-ing, an argument or stalemate. Who is seen as being unreasonable will depend on your viewpoint: as Katherine Whitehorn once said 'I am firm. You are obstinate. He is a pigheaded fool'.

Finally, a deal has to be struck, with both parties wondering 'Have I got you where you want me?' and feeling they have come out of it well.

> Contract: an agreement that is binding only on the weaker party.
>
> Frederick Sawyer

Presentation

It is in this area that the tactical battle of marketing is won or lost. So the way the various presentational activities are selected, and implemented, the appropriateness of what is called the *communications mix*, is crucial.

Think for instance how many varieties of motor oil you can choose to put in your car. There are differences, but many do much the same job at much the same price. To make a choice at all the customer must be influenced by other factors: image, special promotions – something that allows a decision to be made. The final element of choice is often subjective. Because the customer is often faced with similar options, that is much the same sort of product at much the same price, so presentation becomes the marketer's major tool in differentiating his product from others.

So to succeed you must understand and use all the presentational techniques effectively. These are looked at in more detail later.

2

The marketing plan

Planning the attack

Every business needs a plan.

> 'Would you tell me, please, which way I ought to go from here?'
> 'That depends a good deal on where you want to get to,' said the Cat.
> 'I don't much care where . . .' said Alice.
> 'Then it doesn't matter which way you go,' said the Cat.
> 'So long as I get somewhere,' Alice added as an explanation.
> 'Oh, you're sure to do that,' said the Cat, 'if you only walk long enough.'
>
> *Alice's Adventures in Wonderland*, Lewis Carroll

Every management and marketing guru has a version of this or a saying recommending planning. A simple and sensible premise, which any company, any marketer, ignores at their peril.

Plan the work and work the plan is a good motto. It starts by having a clear idea of what business you are in, what the Americans call a 'mission statement'. This is not an academic statement, it can really affect the business. A taxi company will limit itself to taking customers, by road, around town. The more entrepreneurial will go further afield, maybe adding motorbikes to carry messages, but only the company that sees itself in transportation, rather than just taxis, will ever go to the moon.

The plan itself is perhaps less important than the planning. In some companies the plan looks like a telephone directory and takes a team of people six months to prepare, and another team six weeks to circulate and file. Then it sits gathering dust on a shelf and makes little difference to the running of the business. In others the plan is little more than some notes on the back of an envelope, but it does make a difference. It is the *thinking* that goes into planning that makes the difference.

Planning – and thinking – must start with review and analysis. Many marketers use SWOT. This is not some sort of primitive fly killer, but initials standing for: strengths and weaknesses, opportunities and threats. In other words it is simply an approach to looking inside the organization (SW), and outside (OT) to see how well positioned the organization is to develop in the way it wants. Planning must be nothing if not realistic. It is no good planning to go multinational, and then starting by opening a branch office in Paris, if no one in the company speaks a word of French and the French are convinced your brown sauce makes their snails taste horrid. *Zoot alors!*

Not only must planning avoid such disasters, it must inject creativity into the business. It must seek new ways of doing things rather than simply assuming that the company can continue to exploit the market in the same way it always has; anything less will have you doing the equivalent of preparing the marketing plan for expanding telex sales as the email arrives from the receivers.

No business can operate in isolation from the market, so your business plan is your marketing plan. The theory, of course, is that the planned application of sound marketing principles is that simple, even the biggest, best, most assured marketing organization can make the most almighty mess of things.

However by analysing:

- what you want to achieve;

- how far you are towards your objectives;

- how you will take action to implement the plan;

you have a firm basis from which to operate.

Even after careful planning the marketing approach you advocate will still be something of a shot in the dark. There are always unknowns. But any light that can be brought to bear will help, and the consequences of not having enough information are clear; there is all the difference in the world between a light at the end of the tunnel and a train coming towards you. Pessimists make poor planners; seeing any light at the end of the tunnel, their reaction is only to order more tunnel.

Remember, a plan that is only a budget is not enough, the plan must concentrate on *how* things will be achieved, who will do what and not least what will *not* happen. The plan must focus attention and activity on key areas. You can not, indeed must not, try to do every-thing. The extent of the product range provides a good example of this principle. Many companies have far too many products, sometimes doing justice to none because the effort and resources are too thinly spread. Relentless concentration pays off for some; Wrigleys make only one product, chewing gum. But they sell millions and millions of packets of it; as the streets of many a city testify.

Whilst a company can sometimes be successful without a plan, most successful companies do plan, and successful marketing men spend time getting the plan right. They bear in mind the military adage 'time spent in reconnaissance is never wasted', though having laid plans and mounted a successful attack they may prefer to describe what has been done as instant creative decision making, and a reflection of their inherent understanding of the market. You can be a good planner and sneaky.

Product plans

Annual plans for each product are an essential ingredient of any self-respecting marketing plan. On an agreed date, well in advance of the start of the financial year, each product is reviewed in detail, its past progress measured, its future development charted down to the smallest detail. Targets are agreed for sales and profits as well as for the more nebulous aspects of product development like brand image. Plans are discussed and settled, and on January 1st or whenever, the well-oiled machinery swings into action. That is the theory. What *actually* happens?

Since the planning process takes such a long time, it must often begin a good six months before the start of the year being planned. You will therefore have only the first few months' trading results to go on, and will find it difficult to see ahead to year's end, let alone try to pierce the impenetrable gloom of eighteen months. So-called scientific planning, therefore, descends to the level of crystal-ball gazing, nine-tenths of planning is ineffective and frustrated by competition, or simply foiled by outside events. Perhaps all you have to do is to await the inevitable and take the credit for it.

Brand strategies

An integral part of the product plan is a statement of what you want customers to believe about your product and how you will set about making them believe it. You may be appalled by what you take to be the sheer cynicism of the first brand strategy statement you read. Don't let it show. A little reflection will convince you that what you took for hard-boiled cynicism is actually hard-headed realism. You do want the public to believe a lot of things about your product, some of them true, some half-true, some simply half-formed impressions. You are certainly not going to set out to deceive, but you will have to exploit your product's strengths if it is to succeed in the market place. If psychologists have discovered that people associate fast cars with virility then you will do better by giving some mention of this in the promotion.

Having said that, brands are crucial; and *brand image* is as important – if not more important – than the product or service itself. The brand image might be best described as the total personality of the product. It incorporates everything about the product with all the ideas and beliefs the public has about it; all its qualities, real or imaginary, are bound up in it. So important are brands that they can now be regarded as having real value and are assessed as a tangible part of the assets of a company being sold or taken over.

Branding is most readily associated with FMCG marketing, but it is important in every field. The name of a firm may itself be the brand, and any organization needs to consider the associations that go with their name.

Companies often see what they do as *brand development*. This may be done in two ways. First, a company may allow their own name to remain in the background and have a range of products all with different names. Others create a 'family' effect by which the same name appears on a range of products. *Brand extension* can be very successful, for example Mars Ice Cream might not have been so successful if it had not been linked to a successful and known name.

Another aspect of brand strategy is *brand positioning*. This is not the marketing equivalent of the Kama Sutra, but the way in which a brand is 'positioned' to maximize its appeal to a particular sector. Marketers thus talk of 'young' brands (those appealing to young people), 'premium' brands (those appealing to people wanting extra-high quality and prepared to pay for it) and 'female' or 'male' brands. And you need to be sure that your marketing does not fail from trying to be all things to all people in an era when specialization *(niche marketing)* is the name of the game.

Many brands are linked to and use the concept of lifestyle to promote themselves. Their proposition is that buying them and being seen to use them will ensure that you are regarded in a particular way. The approach seems to work, though the credibility of those consumers who really believe their whole life will be changed just by pouring the right concoction down the loo, or eating the right thing at breakfast, boggles the imagination. In fact, such campaigns are not really taken literally. Rather, many consumers enter into the spirit of the thing: they like to imagine that their lives could be different, they find the images fun and thus buy accordingly. Remember: perception is everything.

Branding is powerful stuff and never more so than when it links to fashion. Fashion can arise without the marketing people having anything to do with it. Filofax is an example. It somehow just grew in terms of being a fashionable accessory (marketing built on this and kept the process going). Psion (electronic organizors) have been marketed, in part, on a similar basis, so too Palm personal organizer/ computers which have overtaken them. Or it can be manufactured. People can even be induced to buy brands when no one but themselves is likely to know they have done so. How many people pay a fortune for a necktie with a smart label which will remain firmly against their chest, unable to change the opinion of those who say to themselves: 'Whatever made them buy *that*?'

But planning cannot be only a matter of creating, positioning and extending brands; you have to relate it to some numbers – and to the finances of the business.

Budgets

These are, or should be, inextricably linked to the plan. Both are necessary and a budget pretending to be a plan is not much use.

Budgeting systems can be complex, a wretched superstructure of operating statements and actual/forecast comparisons. Even with only a fairly sophisticated setup, you will find yourself facing an enormous pile of budget documents month by month. For each product you market you will have a sales budget broken out into quarters and, in the current period, into months. You will have a separate budget for sales promotion for each product broken out in the same way, and another for market research. You will also have an operating statement in which achievement is compared against target in terms of profit. The whole lot will probably be put into overall company documents circulated endlessly, filed and refiled; yet it is there to be used, for the important task of monitoring performance if nothing else.

The monitoring process is to measure progress so far, and allow action to be taken to change things if necessary. Targets are there to be exceeded; doing so is important to your credibility. So what do you do when:

Profits are down?

If there is no action you can take in the market to improve matters, then revise the target downwards. That way when the year's results appear, you see, you will be able to claim to have beaten at least your target if not last year's achievement.

Profits are up?

In this case consider revising your target upwards so as to allow a good result in the current year whilst discouraging others from expecting too much of you next year – you want a target you can beat then too.

If things are going really wrong you can always call in a consultant at the last minute, to share the blame.

> Too many crooks spoil the percentage.
>
> H Chandler

May I ask you a few questions?

Many of us are exposed to research at some time or another, but the researcher who stops you in the street with a clipboard in hand and a pleading look on their face is only the tip of the iceberg.

Research can make a key contribution to marketing, and should be especially helpful to planning and decision making. By asking a small number of people their views and inferring statistically what it means to the market as a whole, it provides the marketer with the nearest he will ever have to a crystal ball. It is not, of course, infallible; nor does it remove the need to use judgement, but it is a help.

There are various kinds of research, these include:

- *Market research* questions the use or purchase of a product, asking: who buys? what competitive products are bought? when? where? how much? how often?

- *Product research* measuring the acceptability of a new or revised product: such as whether people will like brightly coloured cornflakes

- *Marketing method research* establishes how customers view your marketing activity, for example, your promotional tactics

- *Motivational research*, inherently more difficult, tries to discover why products are liked or disliked.

- *Attitude research* looks at attitudes to suppliers and attempts to measure such factors as how well the image is put over, or how service levels are perceived.

As political polls show all too clearly, while you can research the past or the present, there is no way to research the future. But people's actions in the past may be a guide to future action so research can provide a useful 'signpost'.

Researcher: someone who can go directly from an unwarranted assumption to a preconceived conclusion.

Anon

Specialist help may be necessary from your research department or a research agency. They, after all, are paid to understand the statistical factors involved, and to know what can be done with *regression analysis* and at least 36.43 other statistical techniques.

Marketers recognize two kinds of researcher. The cynical, who they believe will borrow their watch to tell them the time; and the very cynical who they believe will also keep the watch. In truth, researchers perform a valuable function; after all, identifying consumer need is far too important to leave to customers. To use researchers successfully you must brief them properly. For example in any survey you will only get answers to exactly what you ask; ask people whether they approve of smoking whilst praying and most will say 'no'. Ask whether they approve of praying whilst smoking and most will say 'yes'. Yet both describe the same two things done simultaneously. So check the wording of questionnaires carefully.

If we knew what we were doing it wouldn't be called research, would it?

Attributed to Albert Einstein

Concentrate on specifically what you want to find out, and leave the researchers to worry about *how* they do it. Let them incorporate *depth interviews, hall tests, usage surveys* and the like, though keep an eye on the budget. In their search for statistical perfection researchers are inclined to spend money like it is going out of fashion and it may seem as if they are printing the questionnaires on ten pound notes.

At the end of the day however, research is a good thing. It is good to know as much as you can, even if realistically you cannot be sure of everything; research can act to reduce risk and that is, in fact, the key role it plays in marketing.

> No question is so difficult to answer as that to which the answer is obvious.
>
> George Bernard Shaw

A finger in the wind

Sales forecasting is the art of predicting how much of the product will actually be sold in a given period of time.

Whilst an important part of the annual ritual of budgeting and planning, the only thing that is absolutely certain about sales forecasting is that it will be wrong. What is more, it will be wrong despite an awe-inspiring array of techniques to ensure it is accurate. These include *exponential smoothing*, *econometric models* and *seasonality*, to name but three.

Because it is never possible to calculate the right figure, the final figure that is used is always, in part, guesswork.

Once you have recognized this you can sidestep all the complicated techniques and simply describe your best estimate as the calculated figure. Better still, present it to four places of decimals. This always makes it appear so accurate no one will question it. The great thing with forecasts is to appear supremely confident with them. Put them on computer printout and they assume the certainty of tablets of stone, adding weight to your arguments whilst being a good deal easier to take to meetings.

> He uses statistics like a drunken man uses lampposts – for support rather than illumination.
>
> Andrew Lang

Numerical information can be a powerful ally; remember others will be as confused as you are, or more so. Whoever you are meeting, or trying to persuade, if you really want to keep ahead at least make sure they understand what you want. Many people can read a graph in a way they cannot read tables of figures, so use them to make a point. Amortize, particularly costs, for example, 'less than £100 per month' will secure agreement, where 'about £1200 a year' will sound outrageously expensive.

When you have decided upon your forecast stick to it. Resist the temptation to embellish it. What often happens is this. Marketing makes the forecast, then it is passed to sales plus 10 per cent 'to give them something to go for'. Production are given a figure a little lower than the forecast 'just in case we don't sell that much, and have too much left in stock'. And so on. It all seems very reasonable but accuracy diminishes step by step and suddenly the only thing you can be sure of is being wrong. If the salesmen sell their target figure there is not enough stock; if they only sell the lower figure then you have the stock but they do not hit target and are demotivated. In the light of all these imponderables no one will expect your annual forecasts to be right; and, even if they do, you have a whole year to think of good reasons why completely unpredictable events changed what happened. All of us have 20/20 hindsight.

> NOTICE
>
> The forecasting meeting scheduled for 3pm on 26 March has been cancelled, owing to unforeseen circumstances.

Numeracy

You need your wits about you to deal effectively with figures and statistics. Figures can be made to do almost anything, making them do just that is the statistician's stock in trade. They can be an ally to the marketer, but they can be actually dangerous; witness the statistician who drowned wading across a river with an average depth of three feet.

Everyone in marketing needs an increasing facility with figures. Once upon a time the marketer who made £2 by buying at £10 and selling at £12 thought this was pretty good and that it was amazing how 'that 20 per cent adds up'. The marketer who does this today will make the same amount of money but knows why, even if they need a portable computer terminal, or at least a calculator, to tell them.

A calculator is an invaluable tool for the marketer. It can buy time: you say something like 'let me work out a few figures' whilst actually thinking of what to say next. It can blind with science: 'of course at that level of discount the return you get will be 12.32 per cent', you read off the figure with enormous confidence – it sounds as if it must be right, even if in fact you are guessing.

If you take this sort of attitude research and statistics are fun. There are endless types and varieties to put your wits against and while slide rules have given way to computer spread sheets and the technology of number-crunching gets ever more sophisticated, your judgement and experience will always have a role to play.

Interpreting the figures

Decisions that could once be taken on the nod of a head, and which would have been proved right, or wrong, depending on the wisdom of the particular head involved, are these days likely to be preceded by costly research, volumes of statistics and profusion of raw data.

Decisions are still likely to be right or wrong, depending on who interprets the data and how. And it is now a longer and more costly process. So you must fight your way through the fog of figures, reports, assessments and graphs, and make a decision which takes account of the information in the way you want. There are three approaches:

1. Using the figures

Sometimes the decision you wish to take is supported by the research results and figures available. When this occurs take every opportunity of quoting chapter and verse to uphold the absolute truth of the reasoning behind your decision. You will find yourself in this position so infrequently, it is advisable to make the most of it.

2. Embellishing the figures

More usually your expensive investigation and research ends in a result that can be variously held both to support and oppose the course of action you have in mind. In cases of this sort, everything turns on the interpretation of the raw data. Before your researchers compile their reports (and always insist that the interpretative report is compiled by the researcher) make a point of seeing them and discussing the data. It should not be difficult in a meeting of this sort to show them the way your inclinations lie, and if they have a good head on their shoulders they will march off and compile a first-class interpretative report. It is astounding how, while remaining true to the strict principles of their own profession, they can yet, by devious hints and signs, indicate the essential correctness of the decision you wish to take.

3. Ignoring the figures

This, the most challenging situation, is when the research undertaken is clearly at variance with the action you have in mind. Challenging, yes, but if successfully turned to advantage so very rewarding. Your procedure is to take the experienced marketing man's stand. Whatever the figures say, you can 'smell' the right thing to do. You are going to take the bold step of ignoring research and steering by the seat of your pants.

Here you stand a good chance of pulling off the coup of a lifetime. Ignoring expensive research and being proved right will establish your marketing reputation for many a long year. Ignoring expensive research and being proved wrong however, need not be a disaster, indeed it can be turned into an opportunity by finding or inventing the circumstances that caused the operation to fail. You can then maintain that, basically, your decision was sound, but that 'extraneous factors' worked against it. Taking a stand of this sort is hard the first time but comes easier with practice.

Given the opportunities, you will be astounded at the skill you will eventually develop in explaining away disasters. They say that even the ablest marketing man need only be correct in 51 per cent of his decisions. That leaves 49 per cent where bluff is an essential ingredient.

Juggling with the figures

The world has divided into two groups in recent years. There are those who are 'computer literate' and those who are not. Well three if you consider those, like the author, who hover somewhere in the middle, uncertain whether to join the technological maelstrom or, indeed, whether the brave new world will either have them or allow them to survive in it. At a simple level this book makes a good example. When it was first published I wrote it out by hand – every word – then someone typed it, then I amended it and so on. Since then I have learnt to type. Let me rephrase that: I have become keyboard literate – after a fashion. My keyboard skills could doubtless be better, but I do now input this kind of thing straight onto a word processor; I can even do some clever things like making the text **bolder** and moving thigs arounde * and r%arrangige them (most of the time). Actually I now could not do the portfolio of consultancy, training and writing I do without these skills. Or it would be difficult to do so. Time moves on.

In the area of figures, however, such skills are certainly becoming mandatory. Spreadsheets and other computer devices can show the effect of six different per cent price changes on budgets at the touch of a button; and automatically rework it all in yen or whatever may be necessary. No self-respecting marketer is now without his PC – preferably a laptop, and of the right brand. And some use them unashamedly to bluff those whose new skills are lagging behind.

Something old, something new

Products do not last for ever. Marketers talk mysteriously about the *product life cycle*. Products are born, develop, are nurtured in a mature state, but ultimately, they die. This may take a long time, especially if changes are introduced to resuscitate an ailing product. But it could be a rapid cycle, like a fashionable dress which lasts a season, a pop record that lasts a few weeks.

So product development needs to be a continuous process, and in some businesses a dynamic one. It may seem easy to come up with new ideas – Tupperware Corsets perhaps (slogan, 'They don't make you thinner, but they keep the fat fresh') but will people really buy them? Brilliant new concepts that will create their own markets are not in fact the easiest thing to think up, especially not at the drop of a hat as your current product falters and needs replacing. Take comfort from the fact that most new products are not in fact new at all. They are:

■ adaptations;

■ updates; or

■ variations on a theme.

Sometimes this implies a change which is frankly cosmetic, something like – New Whizzo detergent with added 152M. It still makes your clothes white and your hands red but it sounds ever so much better. Sometimes it means a real improvement, like the first kettle to switch itself off rather than fill the kitchen with steam while you talk on the phone in the hall. Sometimes it seems new, but is it? The ballpoint pen was only a new way of writing, the word processor is only a development of the typewriter albeit with real advantages. Moreover one thing does not necessarily lead to another, as a recent advertisement put it: 'you do not develop an electronic calculator by doing research on the abacus'. Occasionally there is something really new. Xerox and the electrostatic copier is often quoted, but the need for copies was being met hundreds of years before by monks with quill pens. Really new things are rare, so if you have a truly original idea you may well get rich.

> A finished product is one that has already seen its better days.
>
> Art Linkletter

Any new product must meet a need, but people do apparently need the most amazing things and there are companies, and thus marketers, making a good living from selling for instance water, albeit in posh bottles, air, in garages, even canned London fog. Others make their profit from the product we do not use, rather than what we do: how many tons of mustard are left on the sides of British plates even after one Sunday lunchtime and what cost does it represent?

More often therefore you need to inject an element of novelty in the form of a *product plus*; adding an acceptable flavour to medicine to

make it suitable for children; a coloured stripe to toothpaste –
perhaps even one containing something useful like a mouthwash;
or a + grip on the top of a screw.

> If they haven't heard it before, it's original.
>
> Gene Fowler

Product development is a continuous process. While some products
go on for ever – how many can remember a time before Bisto gravy?
– others are here today, gone tomorrow. What price yesterday's
newspaper, unless our picture is in it? Sometimes the gestation
period makes an elephant seem like a fast worker, with something
like a new airliner taking years of development. In some industries
competitors leapfrog each other constantly, so that if your new
product is actually on the market, it is obsolete.

High risk

However new the new product may be, the development process
involved is always risky. The statistics show that nine out of ten new
products fail. Sometimes spectacularly so; the history of new
products is littered with corpses. Remember Strand cigarettes? 'You
are never alone with a Strand' the ad said; great idea, great advertising. No customers. New product development is a veritable
minefield for marketers; there are quite a few of their corpses around
as well. One new product failure is bad enough. They can, at worst,
instigate a domino effect. One particularly spectacular failure of
recent years was the Sinclair C5, the ill-fated electric 'car' which was
described as a hoover-craft or, less charitably, as a grey electric
bedroom slipper. As the launch of this product brought a whole new
meaning to the expression falling flat, those tooling up to make bolt-
on goodies such as roof racks, spoilers and go-faster stripes also had
a disaster on their hands. Perhaps the only people better off for its
demise were the Royal Society for the Prevention of Accidents.

Because so many new products fail, because hundreds of ideas are pondered, sifted and rejected before one goes forward to launch, marketers getting involved in the process are well advised to proceed with caution. If you are careful and can make sure your new product is that one out of ten that succeeds, then the rewards for success are high.

There are three main ways to proceed: risky, very risky and downright foolhardy:

Risky

The most likely way to succeed is with a revised product labelled new, or with what is called a *me-too product*. This latter is where you jump on the bandwagon copying someone else's brilliant idea, particularly if you can improve it a little or make it cheaper. Even when the original product is well established, a new version of the product may succeed in the market, perhaps even take over as leader; as the old saying has it 'the trouble with being a pioneer is that you get shot by Indians'.

A good trick, if you happen to be first in the field with a new product, is to fragment your own market with a me-too product before major competition can get under way.

Very risky

Here you go for a new idea. If it is a good idea it may succeed, but the risks still loom large. Maybe it gets off to a good start but is rapidly overtaken by me-too products; failure of any element of the launch can spell disaster. And if it was really new, demanding expensive development, the loss if it fails can be millions of pounds. Research or test marketing may increase the chances of success.

Downright foolhardy

Backing a hunch, launching a product with no research or test at all, will rarely succeed. But sometimes a hunch does pay off. A new idea launched with no research or test can still succeed. One product reputed to have been launched in this way was the Sony Walkman personal stereo. A clever design plus hunch, no research but it swept the world, spawning a whole generation who know that if the music is not too loud, they are going deaf.

Not least of the problems of working from hunch is that of persuading others within an organization to back it. Asking for £20 million is difficult enough, answering the question 'how do you know it will succeed?' by just saying 'I know' tends to sound a bit thin. Even when the idea is good this can be a problem. Take 'puffa' jackets, or gilets, a very successful product in recent years. But can you imagine the bloke who dreamt up this idea going to his boss and saying 'I've got this great new product idea, a new warm coat for the winter – with no sleeves!' But someone must have done. As a marketer you must not just have the bright ideas but be able to persuade others that you are right. Whatever approach is used the search for, and research to find, new product ideas will no doubt continue as long as marketing persists.

> Scientists discovered a link between silicon and melba toast. After fifteen years of exposure to air, silicon turns into melba toast . . . The findings caused panic amongst computer makers and other businesses that rely on the silicon chip. However, makers of processed cheese spreads were elated at the news.
>
> *Off the Wall Street Journal*

A trial run

Test marketing is one useful approach which does increase the chances of launching a new product successfully.

With this technique, instead of launching your new product on an unsuspecting public across the whole country, you pick a small area and try it there first. The area concerned should be, as far as possible, representative of the country as a whole.

The difficulty lies in finding a suitable area. Luckily there are dozens of agencies, including the independent TV companies, only too anxious to do this for you. All you do is pick one and mount a mini-marketing operation to sell the product in that area alone.

Usually this means a TV region, sometimes a county, occasionally a town. In the unlikely event that researchers can one day show that Arcadia Avenue, Watford is representative, or any individual street, the technique will really reduce costs. The greatest advantage of test marketing is that you succeed whatever happens. If the test goes well and the product sells, you can move on confidently to a national launch. If not, you claim it was only a test and that you have saved the company untold sums of money that would have been lost by going national straight away. So take the credit for that and find another new product – fast.

There is another way in which you can make test marketing work for you. Watch out for your competitors using the technique. If it goes well of course it may affect your product badly.

While you cannot stop your competitors' test market activity, you may be able to reduce its effectiveness. You can play the gentleman and let all run smoothly of course, or you can adopt a more sneaky approach and use a variety of techniques to spoil his game. Try:

- stepping up your own advertising in the area concerned;

- offering trade discounts to stockists;

- launching new promotional activity, free gifts, coupons, money off vouchers.

All this will reduce demand for your rival's product, immediately and in the future, while building your own market share faster than otherwise would have been the case.

Sabotage may not be in the index of most marketing books but that does not mean it does not happen.

Neither launch, nor test marketing are possible without promotional activity so let us turn next to the techniques comprising the promotion or communications mix.

Eighty per cent of success is showing up.

Woody Allen

3

The promotion mix

Blowing your own trumpet

Nothing referred to so far, even the best product, the most carefully prepared marketing plan, the most cleverly set price, guarantees success in the market.

In order to succeed you need to make sure that customers know about your product, indeed not just know about it but are persuaded it is worth buying and, what is more, that it is preferable to competitive offerings. This has always been the case. The Neanderthal axe salesman, referred to earlier, probably put up a sign outside his cave 'Axeheads for Sale'. As competition increased he may have amended it to 'Best Axeheads for Sale' and as competition got fiercer still he would have had constantly to change his approach and become more creative in what he said.

They say if you build a better mousetrap than your neighbour, people are going to come running. They are like hell. It's the marketing that makes the difference.

Ed Johnson

In this modern competitive era more time, effort, and money have to go on communicating with the market. While there are still some people who believe promotion and advertising are unnecessary, this is rarely the case in practice. One diehard managing director dis-covered this to his cost when the first advertising he was persuaded to do was putting a 'For Sale' sign outside his bankrupt factory.

For most, promotional activity is a crucial element of marketing. The question is not whether to do it or not, only how much to do of what, and how to make it persuasive.

And the whole process demands ingenuity to a degree that is perhaps well illustrated by the tale of the three brothers who all opened butchers shops next door to each other. The first put up a sign above his shop which read 'H Smith. Butcher'; the second, two doors away, not to be outdone put up a sign which read 'J Smith. Master Butcher'. The third, more creative brother, strategically situated himself in the shop between the other two and put up a sign which read simply 'Main Entrance'.

The promotion mix

There are, of course, a variety of promotional techniques from TV advertising to mail shots, from posters to hot air balloons, known collectively as the promotion, or communications, 'mix'.

To put together the right promotional mix demands an under-standing of how customers come to make buying decisions, how the various promotional methods work and something about each. A customer must be moved from being totally unaware of the product, first to being aware of it, then to being interested in it, to evaluating its relevance to him, possibly to trial of it, then to usage and with many products to repeated usage. From 'Never heard of it' to 'More, more'.

> There is only one thing in the world worse than being talked about, and that is not being talked about.
>
> Oscar Wilde

Promotional activity has to be carefully designed to lead the potential buyer through this process. Some promotional activity is to provide information, prompt interest and evaluation and so on through to reminders to regular buyers to buy again.

The promotional methods selected must be appropriate. There is a profusion of promotional techniques. For any particular business only some of those available will be right. It is clearly not sensible to promote cosmetics in motoring magazines which are read mainly by men, or offer a free spanner with every lipstick.

Furthermore, promotional activity must be cost effective in proportion to the amount of the product that will be sold. This puts a limit on the sheer volume and the lavishness of what is done. You cannot take each individual customer out by Rolls Royce to the Ritz for lunch as an inducement to buy. Some of the main techniques follow:

Everyone has an image

The question is whether the image is good, bad or indifferent. It will have an impact whatever it is.

Many things contribute to image. The way a telephone is answered, the look of a shop, the style of a letterhead or business card, the design of a logo. Many organizations spend a considerable amount of time and money on such things, which together can have a powerful effect. You might be surprised how many companies which appear to have a modern, thrusting, international image conjuring up pictures of modern offices and factories teeming with efficient activity are in fact a handful of people operating from a shed in Acton.

In fact the right image forms a sound foundation for all promotional activity, and a prime contributor to the opinions customers, and others, have of an organization is *public relations*.

> Only fools don't judge by appearances.
>
> Oscar Wilde

A puss of publicists

The cheerful group noun above, coined no doubt by the same wit who described a group of headmasters as a 'lack of principals', highlights the dark side of public relations, or PR as it is known. And in all honesty there is a dark side, the archetypal publicist, gin and tonic in hand, trying to persuade some innocent journalist that black is white. The word *spin* usually has negative connotations.

Difficult that may be, but an insistent campaign does have an effect and the reason PR is inclined to have a bad name stems from the unsympathetic causes it, from time to time, promotes. If you are on the receiving end, therefore, of a campaign to persuade you that having a railway line through the middle of the house might be a nice change and convenient for commuting, or that a nuclear waste dump in your back garden would allow you to do the world an environmental favour, you may be forgiven for some scepticism about the whole process. Of course it tends to be government, who are not averse to using marketing campaigns when it suits them, who promote such causes. Industry needless to say will have no truck with any such thing.

Positive public relations

So what positively can PR, which embraces a variety of ways of creating and maintaining the right image of the company, achieve? It sets out to influence the climate in which other promotional activity can flourish. It entails liaising with the press and other media, with the intention of getting free mentions in their pages or programmes, and can include other activities as diverse as sponsorship of sporting events or running an advisory service linked to the product, as a baby food manufacturer might do for example.

The net effect should be positive but the PRO (Public Relations Officer) is also the company spokesman when there are problems.

This makes the job of the PRO difficult, to say the least. What do you say to the press when your company has recalled thousands of new cars because their gear-boxes are likely to drop out halfway up the M1? Neither 'Whoops!' nor pointing out what attractive sculptures the bits make when piled up on the hard shoulder sound too good. The Romans used to execute the bearers of bad tidings. Or was it the Greeks? No matter, historical research is beyond the scope of this book. The wise marketer delegates the task, the PRO collects the flack and the marketer's reputation remains unscathed. Perhaps. Maybe this is the origin of the immortal phrase 'No comment'.

Sometimes public relations activity is reactive, that is the opportunities present themselves. For example if you succeed in doing something as novel as obtaining a valuable export order for refrigerators from Greenland, the press may approach your company for a comment. However, like any other promotional activity PR is best planned, press releases must be issued, journalists wined and dined, visits to the factory laid on, in short a whole programme of activity that is designed to keep the firm's or the product's name in front of the market.

It all takes time and effort, but because you are not paying for space as with advertising it can be useful and cost effective. There are dangers occasionally because you do not actually control what is said, or at least what is quoted, in the press. This can make the process less effective than you intended, or even make it backfire. A company issuing a press release announcing a new breakthrough in computer-assisted production techniques may generate a positive mention, or one suggesting they are likely to make unemployment worse.

Another danger is that much of PR relies on personal impact. In some companies it is only when the managing director gets up at a press conference or appears on radio or TV that it is suddenly very clear why money spent on a professional PRO would be well worth while.

Rattling a stick

> Advertising may be described as the science of arresting human intelligence long enough to get money from it.
>
> Stephen Leacock

Advertising is the bit about marketing everyone knows of, some even believing that advertising is marketing. It consists of messages for which you have to pay. On TV, radio, in newspapers, magazines, on posters, even inside taxis or on litter bins. Practically everywhere there are advertisements. From the customers' view there is practically nowhere short of the bottom of a coal mine where there are none. Indeed, if you spot anywhere where there are none it may well be an opportunity to sell the space to someone.

While many smaller, and some larger, companies do their own advertising many more use an advertising agency to do it for them. Agencies spend a lot of time taking each other over and thus acquiring longer and longer names, and more time chasing business. The contract to advertise a particular product is a fragile thing and accounts move from agency to agency in a constant search for a fresh approach. Some time of course has to be spent actually producing advertising and thus guaranteeing the sale of their clients' products.

The advertising agency

Advertising is a highly specialist area of marketing. Advertising agency people are certainly different. Particularly those on the creative side who actually think up the slogans, write the words and design the advertisements. The more creative they are the higher will be their salaries and the less formal their standard of dress, so that the £100,000 a year ad-man is instantly recognizable at a business gathering by his army-surplus denims. (The sort whose large pockets will accommodate the ubiquitous Filofax or, these days, PDA.) However, as even the less creative are at least sufficiently creative to dress the part, a clear hierarchy is difficult to spot.

Choosing an agency can be difficult, therefore large accounts will normally short-list a number and let them put up ideas. It may be difficult not to be censorious but the advertiser is not trying to choose what they like best. Rather what the typical customer will find appealing, and putting themselves in the position of, say, a hard-pressed working class housewife shopping for the week's groceries with two small children and a dog in tow may not be easy if your nearest personal experience is telephoning Harrods and asking them to deliver.

Making it work

Having selected the agency, however, you must consider what advertising can do for you. The most famous saying about advertising is that of the company chairman who said 'I know half the money I spend on advertising is wasted, but I do not know which half.' He was probably right. Advertising is not a science, but however much customers deny it (are you influenced by advertising?) it is a vital part of the promotion and sale of many products. Some campaigns pass into the language. Who cannot still recall such slogans as 'Guinness is good for you', 'Drinka pinta milka day', 'This is the age of the train' and 'Kogan Page Business Books are best'? Sometimes the image and success of a product is transformed. For example it was when research showed people rated gas as a dirty, old-fashioned, inefficient and expensive fuel that Hi-Speed Gas was born. As a result, most people really do now rate gas as a better way of heating their homes and cooking the Sunday roast.

But advertising will not always work exactly as you intend. Sometimes advertising gets too clever for its own good. It may win awards but that does not necessarily mean it will sell the product. It is remembered for the wrong reasons. What was that drink that Leonard Rossiter repeatedly spilt down Joan Collins' cleavage? Do you remember?

Equally advertising is no panacea. It cannot make up for a bad product; whilst it might make a customer buy it once, they will not come back for more if the product is poor. Advertising however is important. The marketer does not of course need to do it all himself, least of all the clever bits – that is what the agency are paid to worry about. He does, however, need to co-ordinate an effective campaign and have a feel for what will work. Bear in mind the key things advertising can do:

It can provide information
Just telling potential customers your product exists is a start. And regular customers need reminding of its continued existence, remember 'out of sight, out of mind' – so the message needs to be regular. The message must say enough to be meaningful. 'Bloggs are best' is of little use unless people know who Bloggs are and what they sell. And it must be clear. There is a surprising amount of ambiguous advertising messages around; how many chemists display a sign saying 'Ears pierced whilst you wait'; there is some other way?

It can persuade

This is the essence of advertising. It is, or should be, persuasive communication. Sometimes the product is such that with no competition, with a perfect match with customers' needs, all the advertisement has to do is say what the product will do for them.

'New instant petrol – one spoonful of our additive to one gallon of water produces petrol at 1p a gallon'. If your message is like this, no problem, persuasion is inherent in the message. But few products are like that. More likely any product will have competition, what is more it will be very like its competitors. Then you have to say more about it. Or start thinking of everything about it. You may even say *everything* about it:

- ■ 'SPLODGE – the big, wholesome, tasty, non-fattening, instant, easily prepared, chocolate pudding for the whole family'.

Or you stress *one* factor, thus implying that your competitors' products are lacking in this respect:

- ■ 'SPLODGE – the easily prepared pudding'.

Customers may know all puddings of this sort are easy to prepare, but they are still likely to conclude yours are easiest. The trouble with this approach is that in a crowded market there are probably puddings being advertised already as 'easily prepared'. And big, wholesome and all the rest for that matter. What then? Well one way out is to pick another factor ignored by your competitors because it is not essential:

- ■ 'SPLODGE – the pudding in the ring pull pack'.

It may be a marginal factor but your advertisement now implies it is important and that competition is lacking. Alternatively you can pick a characteristic of total irrelevance:

- ■ 'SPLODGE – the pudding that floats in water'.

Or link it to the pictorial side of the advertisement:

■ 'SPLODGE – the pudding you can eat on the top of a bus'.

If the competition has done all of this then you have only one alternative, you must feature in the advertisement something else, nothing to do with the product. This may necessitate giving something away:

■ 'SPLODGE – the only pudding sold with a *free* sink plunger'.

Or repackaging:

■ 'SPLODGE – the only pudding in the *transparent* ring pull pack'.

The possibilities are endless and the ultimate goal is always to make your product appear different and attractive, desirable because of it.

It can play on cognitive dissonance

This marvellous piece of jargon refers to the feeling of uncertainty that people can have about the buying decisions they make. Advertising can be explicitly designed to encourage this feeling, casting doubts on past decisions or purchasing habits. Many claims made in advertisements – for example the way Saab cars emphasize their safety – effectively suggest that competitors leave something to be desired in the area described; others go further. Where this approach is used in extreme form it overlaps with what is called *knocking copy*, a clear and sometimes aggressive statement that a competitor is deficient in some way.

It can create reinforcement

In other words it can be designed to reassure existing customers that they are doing the right thing by buying a product. This keeps them coming back for more.

The success of advertising is of course not just a matter of a clever slogan, the whole thing has to hang together. All the copy, the words, in a press advertisement must be good, so must any illustration. On television the attention to detail is apparent in many advertisements. The photography is superb, so much so that it shows up the production of many of the programmes. The music must be right, and music for some advertisements has created hit songs in their own right. Top quality actors are often used, some becoming better known as a character in an advertisement than for their more serious work. In some cases just a voice can make the difference.

The successful totality of all this is difficult to define and ultimately success is only measurable in terms of sales resulting from the campaign.

In addition, what an advertisement can do is influenced by the particular media – where it appears and in what form – used. Each specialist form of advertising is different in approach. You cannot attempt to do what you would in a 60 second commercial on television on a poster.

Media are many and varied. They include:

- *Daily Newspapers* which enjoy reader loyalty and credibility making them a good media. However, they are read hurriedly and can end up wrapping chips within a few hours.

- *Sunday Newspapers* are kept and read longer, but the advertisements tend to get covered in marmalade during lengthy Sunday breakfasts or brunches.

- *Colour Supplements* are kept longer still, and may still be in a pile of various reading matter in the loo a year after publication.

- *Magazines* can be general or specialist. This may or may not be useful. A title like *Octogenarian Hang Gliding* will either be absolutely useless or spot on depending on the product.

- *Local Newspapers* are obviously useful locally, perhaps as part of a test market campaign, with advertisements sandwiched between stories about lost cats and reports on the local fete.

■ *Television* is expensive, very expensive, but undeniably a power-ful medium, though the advent of video is making it more difficult to judge audiences. How many are watching the Saturday midnight movie at teatime on Tuesday week, and skipping the advertisements?

■ *Outdoor Advertising* (posters) is a useful support medium, and useful also on a small local scale, a poster with directions to a local restaurant for instance.

■ *Cinema* is, these days, predominantly for the younger segments of the market, but patrons do usually watch the film – the days of the 'educational' back row having largely gone.

■ *Commercial Radio* is not just TV without the pictures, but attract-ing good creative campaigns in its own right and nationwide there are a lot of stations. If you admit to listening to nothing but Radio 4, try it, it is a revelation.

There is very little these days that does not carry advertising. Marketers have to decide that it is better to put a logo on the side of a space shuttle or use book matches in smart restaurants (those that are not now non-smoking), rather than take a block of space in *Yellow Pages* or paint taxis in their corporate livery. New media come along all the time. Sometimes major changes occur, as currently with the opportunity to have a *Web site* that can be accessed through the Internet. This is still in its infancy. But already it is possible for a consumer to consult a Web site much as they would do a catalogue. Sophisticated software programs allow someone to choose to select which hotel to use by effectively walking through a series of 3-D images on screen. If the system allows orders to be taken, then this process of actually conducting and completing business on the Internet is called *e-commerce*. Every different media has its merits and its disadvantages and selecting the right one is largely a question of understanding consumers, how they live and how they are likely to be influenced when considering a particular category of product.

> If you call a spade a spade, you won't last long in the advertising business.
>
> Anon

Because of the plethora of media available, a necessary skill, at least for marketing many advertised products, is that of *media selection*. This may be a major department in an advertising agency, or be done less formally by an organization without outside support. Either way the job of deciding which side of *News at Ten* a commercial should appear, or whether an advertisement should be placed in one newspaper or another, at which time of year and on which day of the week, is complex. It is also, given the cost of many such media, important. Get it right and your product will sell more. Get it wrong and sales will plummet, though the proprietors of whatever obscure media you have selected will prosper.

After all that has been said, a final comment is worth making. Whatever else it does, and however clever it is, advertising must always be understood. If people do not understand, they do not buy. Well, perhaps it is more true to say that the core message must be understood; after all, what proportion of buyers understand the technical detail of, say, a computer advertisement? The strapline below combines clarity and cleverness admirably.

> Now is the discount of our winter tents
>
> Advertisement at sale time in Stratford-upon-Avon camping shop

> In too many companies, the customer has become a bloody nuisance whose unpredictable behaviour damages carefully laid strategic plans, whose activities mess up computer operations, and who stubbornly insists that purchased products should work.
>
> Lewis H Young

Dear sir or madam

Closely related to advertising is direct mail, much maligned as 'junk mail'. This is actually only advertising that is directed into people's homes or offices on a more personal basis than, say, a poster. It is an effective and fast growing technique, used by large companies and small, and offers great flexibility. A small company might send just ten or a hundred letters (and accompanying material) each week or month; while a large one might mail in tens or hundreds of thousands. Well executed it can bring good, and often easy to measure, results. And the Post Office love it.

Again, it has to be said this is a specialist technique. It is not as easy to do successfully as it might appear – the copywriting particularly must be tailored to the job (and use 'magic words' such as *new, special* or *exclusive* throughout). Bad direct mail (and there is a lot about) will bring in little business and can give the whole technique a bad image. Because of this perhaps, some people object to this, though quite why, when they happily accept that every other page of their favourite magazine is an advertisement, is not clear. But it does work, not everyone throws mail shots instantly away, there are some who read and some who buy. It is an easy media to test and can be very cost effective. Like all advertising the message is important, but so is the list of recipients. Those using direct mail build lists up carefully, guard them from competitors, and in some cases use them repeatedly.

List sources are everywhere. If you take out a magazine subscription, complete a guarantee card, complete the coupon on an advertisement or even write your address on the back of a cheque, expect the post you receive thereafter to increase. And of course overkill does occur and not everything received will be relevant.

Some feel that anyone on the list of a certain credit card company who does not receive three copies of every shot they mail deserves a major prize, particularly if they do not have the card already.

Finally, there is a variety of techniques for measuring advertising effectiveness; these are far too complex to review here and in any case there is only one real way to see what your advertising is doing for you. Stop it. Cancel all your advertising and see what happens. Few are brave enough to try this, so half of all advertising will no doubt continue to be wasted.

> The codfish lays ten thousand eggs,
> The homely hen lays one
> The codfish never cackles
> To tell you what she's done.
> And so we scorn the codfish,
> While the humble hen we prize,
> Which only goes to show you
> That it pays to advertise.
>
> Anon

2p off etc

One of the animals the fictitious Dr Dolittle talked to was the 'Push me pull you' which had a head at each end. This might make a good mascot for advertising and promotion because if advertising is designed to pull the customer to the product, *sales promotion*, the other major area of promotional activity, is there to push the product towards the customer. Promotions which include a plethora of schemes: money off, two for the price of one, coupons valid against future purchases, extra product free and so on, are essentially short term. You put in a promotion to sell things now, rather than later.

Some are aimed at the customer at home, some in the store; at the industrial buyer or the retailer to persuade him to stock more.

Timing is important to all promotional schemes. They need planning ahead and co-ordinating. The marketer who ends up with a warehouse full of toothpaste packed in boxes shouting 'free toothbrush' and no toothbrushes, or whose free beachball promotion is held up until November, is in trouble. Next summer is a long way off and 30,000 beachballs cannot be hidden in the cupboard under the stairs. If you incur the costs and reap none of the anticipated additional sales it is a very visible kind of mistake. One which managing directors are apt to notice.

So you will need to consider carefully the kind of schemes you use and plan their implementation carefully. What works best? Well there are far too many kinds of promotion for any marketer to know them all, much less be able to use them all. You should start with a few, add to them, use them in combination and always vary their form just sufficiently for them to appear new to both your customers and your boss; especially when you pinched the idea from someone else. Here are three for you to start with:

1. Self-liquidation offer

The promotion that costs you nothing. 'Buy three of our product and you receive vouchers enabling you to buy a solar powered calculator worth £10 for only £4.50' says the promotion. As you buy the calculators in bulk in Hong Kong for £2, even the administration and despatch costs are paid for. Sounds great, always provided your customers actually want yet another calculator and the sun shines sufficiently to make it work.

2. Dealer-loader

A promotion aimed not at the ultimate customer but at a 'dealer', a shop or a wholesaler for instance. This is so called because it literally off-loads the manufacturer's stock and loads up theirs. It can take the form of cutting prices to the trade in return for a bigger order, more display space or sale support.

Or you can give prizes or bonuses to the dealer or his sales staff. Experienced shoppers may spot the eager retail salesman with his eye on a major prize, and over-recommending one particular brand.

He may not earn much from selling one gas cooker, but sell fifty and he may end up in Miami. On some foreign beaches every second person you meet is the recipient of some free offer or other.

3. Free offer

This kind of promotion may cost money. The trick is to make the free gift you offer your customers seem worth more than it really is, making it so attractive that it is paid for by the extra sales revenue the campaign creates. Plastic daffodils have rather had their day. Choose a gift people want and ideally something linked logically to your product – in the way that champagne glasses go with petrol. For whatever reason glasses have long been a popular petrol promotion, often giving a free glass with as little as 10 gallons of petrol. At 30 miles per gallon over 25,000 miles per year (and no self-respecting marketer can keep in touch with his customers driving less) that is the best part of 100 glasses! Who drinks all that champagne? But we digress.

Above all you need to dream up imaginative ideas for such offers. How about a free budgerigar with every packet of birdseed, or a free first aid kit with every electric saw? Better still, give away your own product. This is less costly and may help get rid of any surplus stock. Offer two for the price of one or complimentary products such as a free conditioner with a shampoo. Done well this promotes trial use, done badly customers think your shampoo *needs* a conditioner.

Cynical marketers, and perhaps their customers also, reckon there are three kinds of promotion:

■ the creative;

■ the successful;

■ the vast majority.

Marketers who come up with some of the very small minority that are both creative and successful ensure their reputation is made. Failing that they must find an agency that will come up with schemes that are creative and successful for them, and let them take the credit for them. This helps reputation but makes you vulnerable; it may be best to double the time spent in the bath, where all the best ideas occur, and keep on thinking. Anyway, it worked for Archimedes.

A word from our sponsor

Sponsorship is much used and comprises of two levels of activity. First, by associating a brand with an event of some sort (usually sporting or artistic: like the Coca Cola Cup) various promotional techniques can be used in a way that ties in with the event. Much of this is large scale, national or international, and a company may choose to sponsor a major worldwide event (in the way that *Swatch* did as timekeepers to the last Olympic Games). But it could be smaller scale with a minor, or less widely popular, sport being picked or something like a one-off concert being the recipient. This puts money into the event or organizer in return for permission to advertise – and often collaborate in – via the event: in the sports stadium, in the programme etc.

Secondly, on a smaller scale, it gives the company a focus for corporate entertaining, for example, when customers or distributors view Wimbledon from the sponsor's box. Of course, different events lend themselves to sponsorship in different ways. It is possible to imagine gliding down the river at Henley and talking some shop, but with a football match in full voice all around you conversation is inevitably going to suffer. Often the choice is led more by the sponsor's enthusiasm than by hard-nosed marketing considerations.

Good relations

Much of the promotional activity so far described has a dual role: attracting new customers and encouraging others to continue buying. Being remembered is crucial. And not only do customers forget – 'What *was* the name of that company?' – but you have to combat the constant attempts of your competitors to *make* them forget and buy from them. So important is it to keep in touch that a special form of marketing addresses just this problem: *relationship marketing*. Again a plethora of techniques are involved. Often a *database* is important (some talk also of *database marketing*); you do actually need to remember and record who your customers are. Then such devices as brochures, newsletters and sometimes personal contact, from a salesperson calling or telephoning to a promotional event, seminar or demonstration, are used to prevent your name slipping out of the customers' minds. Every customer – existing or past (the latter are sometimes called *dormant*) – may be a potential source of future revenue, even that difficult Mr Richard who expects you to spend your entire day on his modest, and inevitably non-standard, order; but remember no customer is worse than no customer, and keep in touch.

Show off

As a last example of the variety of promotional method, consider *exhibitions*. In many product or service areas the industry or 'trade fair' is a regular element in the promotional calendar. Indeed one of the first trips a copy of this book will make is to the Frankfurt Book Fair, the Mecca of the publishing world; here I confidently expect the rights for translation into a dozen languages and for a mini series to be sold, but I digress (though I trust you are paying attention, Editor).

Exhibiting at exhibitions sounds fun. A few days out of the office, somewhere nice – Cannes perhaps – a gin and tonic in hand chatting up the punters; no sweat. Wrong. Exhibitions are hard work. Setting them up and attending them (they are more likely to be in Coventry than Cannes) is hard on the feet, the stomach and the nerves. On the other hand it can be a good way both to meet new prospects and renew acquaintances with old ones, provided it is well done. There is more to it than handing out a photocopied fact sheet and saying: 'Do give us a call if you are interested'.

Exhibitions can work well, but contacts have to be followed up – the hard work really starts once the team are back in the office – and much of the effort will fall on stony ground. You only have to look at the rubbish bins at the end of an exhibition to see that many of the brochures distributed do not even make it out of the door.

The list of possible promotional methods is almost endless, from Tupperware-style parties to advertising on hot air balloons and bus tickets. Both the methods and the execution of them must be approached creatively, individually and together; it is the orchestration of the mix as much as how individual techniques are handled that makes the total effort effective.

This leaves the vexed question of *how much* promotion should be initiated and what should be spent on it. Promotional budgets can potentially make even a small black hole look anorexic.

Think of a number

So, now you must decide how much money you will spend on all this promotional activity. Some companies spend millions. One TV commercial at peak hours can cost tens of thousands of pounds (that is a thought to ponder as you wander off during the commercial break to make the tea, think of the money some optimistic marketer has spent – the least you can do is watch). In other industries the budget is small; whatever it is the figure has to be decided upon. You could take it off the back of a bus, but this may be dangerous, someone might just ask how you arrive at it. There are luckily some formulae which help you arrive at a figure.

Rule of the thumb

If you spent 10 per cent of sales revenue last year then you can logically spend the same next. Or more. Or less. And what will next year's sales revenue be anyway? Alternatively you can base it on a fixed sum per unit sold, though you may encounter the same sort of problems.

Copycat

If you can find out what your main competitors spend you can match it. Or spend more. Or less. The blind leading the blind again?

Piggybank

What can you afford? Work out the rest of the budget and see what is left for promotion and advertising. This sounds easy but sometimes it suggests nothing should be spent on promotion!

Experience

The best guide to the future is the past, so you can look at what was spent last year, how it worked, what was sold and calculate a formula from that relating it to next year's plans. This stops mistakes being repeated. Until you remember the old proverb 'The reason history repeats itself is that no one listens the first time.'

Task

This is perhaps best, if demanding the most work. Analyse the present situation, set objectives, identify the promotional tasks, cost them out and arrive at a figure.

Better still mix all these methods; adopt the task method, but also keep an eye on competition, last year's situation and what you can afford. Easy, is it not? You will then have a budget enabling you to conduct an overall programme of promotional and advertising activity, half of which will work well. Perhaps. Keep your fingers crossed, and, when it does go well, circulate the results widely; you do not want people thinking that the market share went up all on its own.

The ultimate objective

By dissecting the overall promotion process and looking at what each element of it is and how it works, there is a danger of the overall co-ordinated nature of it being obscured. The promotional mix is exactly that – a mix. Whatever activities are undertaken they must act together to create an appropriate image and prompt sales. To do so activities cannot be viewed entirely independently, nor crucially can results be assessed only one by one. The overall aim of promotion is to create a *dialogue* with the market. This should be an ongoing dialogue, one that changes and develops as one message builds on another towards points at which customers buy; beyond that it continues and, if it works well, customers keep buying. Always it must reflect the real, and changing, situation of markets and competition.

4

Selling and sales management

The second oldest profession

There is an old saying that 'nothing happens until someone sells something'. True enough. No matter how good the planning, advertising and so on are, success will not follow unless the sales element of the mix is right. The final link in the marketing chain is personal. Often one to one, it is the representative calling on retailers, the technical salesperson or sales engineers calling on industrial buyers. They must sell, and sell just the right amount.

There is a story of a customer in a delicatessen who asks for a packet of sugar. 'Certainly' says the shopkeeper and turns to where an entire wall is packed with sugar from floor to ceiling. 'My word, you must sell a lot of sugar' says the customer, 'No,' replies the shop-keeper 'we sell very little sugar. But the guy who sells me sugar, now he sells sugar!' A salesman fired with enthusiasm perhaps, but selling too much can create disgruntled customers. Another customer tells of being sold a retirement policy by an insurance salesman, 'I pay regular premiums for 10 years, then *he* can retire!'

On the other hand if the salesperson sells too little the company goes bankrupt, in which case the salesperson perhaps *should* be fired with enthusiasm.

So selling is a part of marketing and in a competitive environment has to be as professionally carried out as any other marketing technique. The modern salesman is, generally speaking, a professional. But the image of selling lags and it is not, in all honesty, universally thought of as entirely respectable.

In past years, selling collected something of a bad image; and is still regarded by many as not quite nice. Such feelings are prompted by the fear of being sold a pup. And with some justification. Over the years many pups have been sold, and in some industries selling retains this image. If their daughter comes home and announces she is to marry, let's say, a double glazing salesman or someone in the second hand motor trade, many people's first reaction is to lock up the silver. And some would not be that generous.

Nowadays, because of consumerism, legislation, competition and common sense, selling has become, for the most part, respectable. The world, or rather Greenland, is not in fact full of furious Eskimos who have been sold refrigerators they do not want and, while there are no doubt some households which have ever so slightly too many plastic containers, most salesmen provide choice to their customers, identify their needs and sell appropriate products in a professional manner.

So selling is a good thing. Indeed, production without selling is a nonsense; jobs, wages, wealth all come from the right product being sold at the right time, place, price. The salesman by implication is an important person. And what exactly is selling? It is personal, persuasive communication usually on a one-to-one basis. And of course it is easy. Did you ever meet anyone who admitted to being a bad driver, a bad judge of people? Never. Selling is the same. Many feel there is nothing to it, at least given 'the gift of the gab'. It is merely commercial chatting up and you are either a born salesman or not. If you are then, all things considered, it is a pretty cushy way to earn a living, with a nice car, commission and lots of independence.

> To sell something, tell a woman it's a bargain; tell a man it's deductible.
>
> Earl Wilson

This is not of course really true. Professional salesmanship is a complex business. It can be, indeed must be, learnt and, once learnt, constantly fine-tuned to make sure that skills are always used to best effect in an ever-changing market. What is true is that the good salesperson can make it look easy. How? Like anything else, because he knows the tricks of the trade and how to use them.

There are many misconceptions about salesmanship and the characteristics that make a good salesperson. Today's salesman is as likely to look like a senior executive, an engineer or the managing director as the archetypal wide boy. And of course many salesmen are women. What is more, the very nature of the job, or at least certain aspects of it, is in direct contradiction with some elements of the traditional image.

Tradition insists that salespeople are extrovert, they have the 'gift of the gab'. Yet selling is a lonely job. Salespeople may spend only a small proportion of their time, perhaps a quarter or less, actually face to face with customers. So what, you may well ask, do they do the rest of the time? Well much of it they spend in the car, driving from customer to customer with only Radio 1, Jimmy Young or Woman's Hour for company. (As a result salespeople are an infallible source of information on how to cure nappy rash and some, the attentive listeners, will know 26 different things you can do with yesterday's mashed potato.) They also spend time looking for somewhere to park, looking for telephone boxes that have not been vandalized, and waiting – in traffic jams, in reception areas, and whilst buyers speak on the phone or talk with other salespeople.

Some of this time can be put to good use, either in researching customer information, chatting up the buyer's secretary or learning Italian.

So salespeople have to be independent, patient, and good listeners and also good at presenting their case and creating a suitable rapport with the buyers.

Buyers are a tough lot

Many buyers are at least as professional and well trained these days as the salespeople they have calling on them; sometimes more so.

All buyers need to be treated with respect. In many industries major customers are very powerful. Some companies find some 80 per cent of their sales going to 20 per cent of their customers. (This 80/20 rule – Pareto's law – is something every marketer worth his salt has in his vocabulary.) Clearly such major buyers are especially important. For example the proportion of grocery products sold through the major supermarket chains makes their buyers crucial to companies selling in that market.

It is any buyer's job to get the best possible deal for his company. That is what they are paid for, they are not actually on the sales-people's side, and will attempt to get the better of them in every way, especially on discounts.

This is well illustrated by the apocryphal story of the fairground strongman. During his act he took an orange, put it in the crook of his arm and bending his arm squeezed the juice out. He then challenged the audience, offering £10 to anyone able to squeeze out another drop.

After many had tried unsuccessfully, one apparently unlikely candidate came forward, he squeezed and squeezed and finally out came a couple more drops. The strongman was amazed, and, seeking to explain how this was possible, asked as he paid out the £10 what the man did for a living. 'I am a buyer with Ford Motor Company' he replied.

Buyers are not really like this; they are worse. With many different kinds of sales job to be done companies must find the kinds of people best able to influence buyers in the kind of customer to whom they sell.

The different jobs demand rather different skills, qualifications and characters. Some are too obvious to mention. Most salespeople must be able to drive a van or a car, yet more than one company has hired people first and found out that they could not drive (or were banned perhaps) later. No question is too obvious to mention in recruiting these key people.

Always certain skills will be crucial. The sales task of launching a new product or opening new accounts in a difficult market needs a surfeit of persistence, and a thick skin – some customers have more descriptive responses than 'No, thank you'. One salesman tells of finally arriving at a meeting with a prospect he had found very difficult to get to see. 'You should feel honoured' says the prospect 'I have refused appointments with twelve salesmen like you already this week.' 'I know' replies the salesman 'I'm them'.

The person selling computer equipment may need a specific level of mathematical ability. The person selling fertilizer to farmers will need a stout pair of wellington boots, because as one salesman put it delicately: 'Smell it, most days I am up to my knees in it.' Others may need specific academic qualifications, a graduate chemist perhaps being better at selling pharmaceutical products to doctors than his less qualified colleague. Not that qualifications of any sort guarantee an ability to be able to sell anything to anyone. The world is full of graduates who could not sell jelly babies to starving children.

The 'ideal' salesperson

So while the modern professional salesperson does not have to conform to any particular mould, not even driving a Ford Mondeo is mandatory these days, he does need to have three key characteristics if he is to be successful.

The first is the ability to sell, the second is the ability to sell and the third is – the ability to sell! Of course selling involves a plethora of techniques, and a host of approaches, many described in jargon terms: opening and closing, talking benefits, handling objections (for example using the boomerang technique: '. . . it is *because* it is so expensive that . . .'), all of which can be summed up as persuasive communication based on an understanding of customer needs. This implies salespeople must not be condescending, or talk down to customers. (You do *know* what condescending means, don't you?) Put more simply, selling is helping people to buy. For a detailed review of how to make sales techniques effective see my book *101 Ways To Increase Your Sales* (Kogan Page), an excellent and practical treatment of the topic which . . . enough, consider it recommended (if a book about marketing cannot contain an unashamed 'plug', what can?).

Unfortunately for management there is no test guaranteed to identify this ability in advance. And even when the ability is there, what is in fact a complex social skill can actually get worse with practice! This is not as silly as it seems. Salespeople's skills are subject to constant attrition by customers, especially those who say no. So they start to play it safe, build up bad habits and take their eye off the ball. Such skills must be forever fine-tuned so that selling remains effective.

Then the aim must be to see salespeople as marketing's storm troopers, operating at the front line in the market place and contributing an important differentiating factor between the company and competition. A company sales team of grey people, neither good enough to keep nor bad enough to dismiss, will dilute marketing effectiveness and can damage customer relations for a longer time.

All salespeople should be among the company's greatest optimists, certainly on the marketing side of the organization. Perhaps their most important asset is positive thinking. This is well illustrated by the old story of the two shoe salesmen sent out to explore export markets amongst the islands of the Pacific. One cables back REGRET NO ONE HERE WEARS SHOES. STOP. RETURNING AT ONCE. The other sends the message NO ONE HERE WEARS SHOES. STOP. SEND ALL AVAILABLE STOCK.

Salespeople who see the glass as half full, rather than half empty, provide any company with a head start.

Just one more step

It is easy to see the sales job as simplistic: one arm-twisting meeting and sign here. In fact, salespeople have to work at a range of contacts making up the *sales process*. This starts with the identification of prospects and may involve what are called 'cold' calls. These may be made in person or over the telephone. Cold calls are hard work, the strike rate, calling on people out of the blue (even when based on some research), is low. Psychologically they can be draining and it is not everyone's cup of tea. Often completely cold calling is not necessary. First contact may be primarily with people who have made an enquiry.

Even when the prospect is 'warm', selling needs considerable skill. Salespeople must inform, do so persuasively and, at the same time, differentiate themselves, their organization and their product from competitors. It is a challenging task of communication. Well conducted, one meeting may be sufficient to agree a deal. Often this is not the way a customer wants to play it. They make an enquiry, study the literature sent out, have a meeting, want details in writing (a written proposal or quote), then maybe another meeting, samples, a demonstration and a formal presentation to their Board. Throughout this sequence of events there are long silences, or would be if the salesperson did not keep in touch and prompt renewed contact, thus adding to the tasks included in the sales role. And at the end of all this the customer says, 'I'll think about it.' More time goes by, more nudging is necessary until finally the salesperson secures an order – 'Yes!' No wonder they get excited about it. Maybe they deserve their commission.

The sales job thus varies a good deal depending, not least, on what sort of sequence customers go through. Selling to a supermarket is not the same as selling, business-to-business, to a major industrial giant or a one-man business. Not only does the industry prompt differing approaches to the sales job, not least in the knowledge salespeople must have, so too does the size of the customer.

Not just bigger, different

All customers are individuals, of course, and must – and expect to – be treated as such. But there are other differences too; some customers are different from others by virtue of their size. These are not simply bigger, they are different in nature, and need different methods to handle them. First, they have considerably more power – and know it and use it. When your largest customer says: 'Another month's credit would be good,' the immediate fear is of a significant percentage of your business disappearing unless you agree.

Big customers have different expectations and make different demands from smaller ones, and thus need different handling and servicing. This is not just a question of an individual buyer being a bit heavy. Major customers may wield a great deal of power. For example, in Britain five main supermarket groups sell almost all the grocery products supplied to customers. A manufacturer who does not supply one such group is not so much disadvantaged, as dead. On the other hand, such a chain not supplying a leading product is going to lose sales. As the two parties circle around each other, the balance of power shifts to and fro and everything about the product and how it is marketed is part of the way in which the two finally agree to do business. Pricing and promotion, even packaging, may reflect discussions between the retailers and manufacturers rather than being the sole decision of, say, the brand's Product Manager.

Major customers need sensitive handling. Hence, at this level, the breed of salespeople with titles such as *Major (or Key or National) Accounts Executive/Manager*. It is their job to keep this unruly group happy, yet retain some semblance of profitability despite their demands. This is no easy task. Get it right and a major proportion of the company's sales will be assured, for the moment.

Big Customers, big systems

To assist with the process of handling major customers, a variety of techniques have been pulled together into a process known as *customer relationship management* (CRM). Computer systems can help keep track of order patterns, levels of profitability – and ensure that the account executive does not forget the buyer's birthday. The proportion and thus the volume of business originating with major customers – and what is therefore hanging on creating, maintaining and developing constructive and profitable business relationships with them and developing the strategies to do so – make this an area for serious attention. No system can do the job on its own. The responsibility at the end of the day is with the designated sales-person. A lot is hanging on their being good operators; and a good deal of business must be lost because they are not regarded as being as important as they actually are to the business.

If all else fails . . .

Sometimes it has been known for one form of selling to be used, that of bribery. A free pen with the supplier's logo on is one thing, indeed I have one on my desk from my accountant – what is more respectable? Cars, holidays or boxes full of fivers are quite another. Yet for a major contract, or a large overseas order, who knows? However, for a small adjustment to his royalty, the author has agreed to point out that such practice can be illegal and is something with which no aspiring marketer should be involved.

OVERHEARD

1st Salesman: 'I made some very valuable contacts today.'
2nd Salesman: 'I didn't get any orders either.'

Directing the storm troopers

Good marketers take their sales team seriously. They make sure they are well managed, and that control over those on the team is carefully balanced. Too much control and initiative and creativity is stifled, too little and salespeople end up taking orders from no one. So what makes a successful salesmanager? Sometimes a successful salesperson, promoted as reward for their sales success. But the jobs are quite different and success in one by no means qualifies anyone for success in the other. In truth there are a lot of rotten salesmanagers around because of this; as a result of their background they spend a lot of time selling themselves and thus leave their sales team very much on their own.

Lucky salespeople? Well not necessarily: a good salesmanager should be an asset to any salesperson; they are there to achieve results through their team not for them.

Salesmanagers have the six key tasks of planning and organizing the team and the way it works, recruiting people who can and will sell, developing them so that they are always able to perform effectively, motivating them and controlling their activities.

The salesmanager has a complex and important job. It will involve many individual tasks varying from the use of regression analysis to prepare the sales forecast (if you do not know what regression analysis is look it up, you do not get lessons on statistical techniques included in a volume as inexpensive as this one) to checking the salesmen's expenses. All come into the six overall tasks mentioned earlier:

■ *Planning* is a grand word for a little purposeful thought before action. Good managers do their homework, as the old military adage has it 'time spent in reconnaissance is never wasted'. In wartime it may keep you out of danger, in this context it increases the danger of the team making more sales.

It should imply considerable thought about how selling is to take place, the nature of the sales task, which customers are to be visited (and those not to be). It should also no less imply the simple planning premise of engaging the brain before the mouth, and making sure the salesmen do likewise. Planning may seem obviously common sense, but many salesmen started their careers at a time when this was by no means universally accepted.

One old timer reports being recruited to sell invoicing systems. He was given a sample case, a copy of *Yellow Pages* and pushed out onto the streets. He spent three days knocking on doors without getting into one meeting. Then someone took pity on him. He launched eagerly into his spiel, quoted every virtue of invoicing systems he knew, and was then asked if he knew what business the customer was in. He admitted he did not. The customer then declared that he was in shipbuilding; if he issued one invoice a year that would be good. No sale, but such a start led to rapid learning amongst those who survived the experience.

■ *Organizing* such factors as how many salesmen to have on the team, how to deploy them around the country, and how often to visit customers is also an important task. Long hours burning the midnight oil surrounded by maps, pins to show customer locations, and lists of actual and potential customers, trying to decide whether Brighton or Chichester is best covered by the salesmen for the South East or South West, is just the sort of task a newly promoted salesmanager takes in his stride.

■ *Recruitment*, now that is surely a lot easier. It may seem so, everyone likes to think they are a good judge of character. Not so.

The salesmanager who recruits by placing an advertisement requesting applications from people who are 'enthusiastic, self-motivating, personable, persuasive and who respond to a challenge' may well be surprised just how many people believe they qualify. And if they go on to screen candidates by rejecting all those who are less than six feet tall, have double barrelled names or wear suede shoes; and believe they can spot, by instinct or ESP, those who can sell as they walk through the door, they will almost certainly be wrong. Having said that of course if you pick Sagittarians (nature's aristocrats and successful at everything) then recruitment really is easy. Alternatively a careful, systematic approach and sufficient time may be much more likely to succeed.

> Recruitment is easy. Find and appoint a good candidate. Watch and wait to see if they perform satisfactorily. If their performance proves unacceptable – don't appoint them.
>
> Overheard (quoted in *Hook your audience*,
> *Management Pocketbooks*)

■ *Developing* the team is perhaps the most important task of sales management; as the old saying has it 'if you can't train, you can't manage'.

Whilst sending people on courses may sometimes be useful, on-going development implies a process of counselling and demands that salesmanagers spend time in the field working with people individually to improve performance.

Like so much else in marketing, it takes time, but it is important because selling is essentially a *dynamic* process. Becoming proficient at selling is not like learning a more static skill. Set out to learn to juggle with flaming torches and, once you stop burning holes in the carpet and frightening everyone within a radius of 100 metres then you can, with a little practice, consider yourself a qualified juggler. Selling, however, must relate to the market and the customers *as they are now*. Customers' expectations must be met and these do not remain the same. Anyway, customers are not on the salesperson's side, and it is true to say that sales excellence may actually *decline* with practice as defensive habits designed to save face take over from potentially more persuasive techniques. So anyone for whom selling is part of the job must spend a lifetime fine-tuning the way they go about it to make sure that their techniques continue to be appropriate and give them the edge on competition. Perhaps sales development is the marketing equivalent of painting the Forth Bridge.

■ *Motivation* is similarly important, perhaps to everyone, but especially to salespeople who must spend much of their time out of touch with their company in the field. Salespeople must not only be *able* to sell they must *want* to do so. And go on and on doing so.

A host of things make for the right motivational climate, from tangible things like what car the sales team are issued with to the occasional 'Well done' or 'Thank you'. This latter is perhaps the cheapest, and often most neglected aspect of motivation.

Once upon a time all management was a question of 'carrot and stick', less so now. Sticks are out of fashion and harder to find and recent employment legislation means miscreants need influence in the boardroom to get themselves fired.

Sales incentives do however provide a carrot for salespeople. Incentives should not be confused with commission which implies more a reward for work done in the past. Incentives are designed to motivate, to urge the sales team to greater efforts in the future. They may take the form of money, or offer gifts, holidays and, in some companies, even things like the use of the company Rolls Royce for a week or a month. Next time someone pulls up to you at traffic lights and you look across and think 'However can he afford a Rolls Royce?', well, there is a reason. A note of caution: one person taking an increasing interest in these schemes is the tax man. Three weeks in Miami as a reward for record sales may be assessed as a benefit in kind, and be promptly followed by a tax bill.

The best incentive schemes are simple. No one is motivated by spending hours slaving over a hot calculator just to find out how they are doing. Charting results by league tables and score keeping will focus attention on them, and make them more effective.

There are also quite different incentive schemes that would by no means by described as providing benefits in kind. One such is called 'planned insecurity'; every month the salesperson who is bottom of the league is fired – to encourage the others.

> Your motivation is your pay packet on Friday. Now get on with it.
>
> Noel Coward (to an actor)

■ *Control*, last but by no means least, is the task that the salespeople often notice most. Remember that they are out and about on their own 90 per cent of the time. Salesmanagers want to know what they are up to and some will go to surprising lengths to find out, sending out spies to call at their salespeople's homes at the end of the afternoon to feel their car bonnet. If it is cold then they got home too early and did not do a full day's work.

More usually they expect salespeople to submit plans, reports and more reports each week, each day, until it feels, to the salespeople, like on the hour every hour. Often this paperwork seems to disappear into a bottomless pit, no one acknowledges it and nothing more is ever heard of it. If any salesperson is concerned and wants to check, after all, his deathless prose might in fact be able to contribute substantially to the success of the business, nothing could be easier. They simply include something outrageous on the next report, for instance, reporting that they called on Browns' Widgets Ltd, propositioned the receptionist, insulted the buyer, left the sample case behind and knocked down their factory gate post with the car as they left. If they hear nothing, particularly if Browns' Widgets is a good customer, then no one reads their reports. If they do hear something of course they will probably be out of a job and will not therefore need to write any more reports. If all the reports are like that and no one has ever commented then not only do the salesperson and his company have problems, so do the customers.

The swindle sheet

And, finally, back to a task mentioned earlier: checking expenses. The sensible salesmanager wants no hassle with this, he sets down guidelines, checks what goes on and descends like a ton of bricks on anyone trying to beat the system. In most companies therefore it is now quite difficult to finance your hobby or your mistress off expenses; remember the old rhyme:

> In Brighton she was Brenda,
> She was Patsy up in Perth,
> In Cambridge she was Candida
> The sweetest girl on earth.
> In Stafford she was Stella,
> The pick of all the bunch,
> But down on his expenses,
> She was Petrol, Oil and Lunch.

Despite this many salespeople regard expenses as a challenge, constantly seeking to come out on top. Technically, if anyone files fictitious expenses it is theft; and you cannot really have degrees of honesty, you are either honest or not. But it was ever thus, human nature being what it is, salespeople will probably always view expenses as a challenge and in years to come companies selling mining equipment amongst the moons of Jupiter will have sales-managers checking oxygen cylinders used on the trip in the way their present-day counterparts check petrol costs.

> Anyone who lives within their means suffers from a lack of imagination.
>
> Lionel Stander

The travelling 'field' salesperson, moving from customer to cust-omer whether those customers are retailers or industrial buyers, undertakes a considerable range of selling tasks. These range from that of highly qualified technician or advisor to simple merch-andiser, but the process of selling is much more widely deployed by many a marketing orientated company than that, much of the time in ways which may not be immediately fully recognized as such by the customer.

For instance, the bank manager who says 'Of course we could help arrange the mortgage (or insurance) . . .' is selling; the politician asking for your vote is selling. The travel agent, booking the holiday who says 'Can I organize travellers cheques for you . . .' is also selling; so is the barman asking 'Another drink, Sir?' or 'A large one?' and the waiter who asks 'Are you ready for dessert?'

Indeed everyone does have something to sell. Watch out for it. Try it, next time you want to persuade the traffic warden to leave your car alone; or when you say 'Why not come back to my place?' You are selling.

> Everyone lives by selling something.
>
> Robert Louis Stevenson

Thank you for your support

All the good promotion and selling in the world is useless if other aspects of company activity do not support it. Without everyone's contribution to what has become known as *customer care*, other persuasive inputs can be quickly diluted.

Marketing must ensure appropriate service standards are set; this is one area of marketing where *benchmarking* – initiating action after careful comparison with standards achieved by competitors – is sometimes used. It must also ensure that ongoing customer care approaches are an automatic part of the system, and that all individual one-to-one customer contacts consistently not only do the job *customers* want, but that they surpass their expectations; and deliver *excellent service* (what may be referred to as the 'Wow!' factor). Obvious this may be, but service standards can be a weak link in the chain linking company and customer. And excellence is easier to talk about than to achieve.

> *The key rules of superior service*
>
> *Rule 1:* The customer is always right.
> *Rule 2:* If the customer is wrong, refer to Rule 1.
>
> Sign seen in shop

Everyone who has direct customer contact, and many who work in the background, are involved, and can help build the company's image for quality and customer service. Yet, despite the fact that this is obvious common sense, prevailing standards are not high.

Everyone has had contact at one time or another with the switchboard operator who transfers your call five times and makes it seem like your fault. Or been into a company's reception area to find a cold, bare room, one stained table and a broken ashtray for furniture, yesterday's newspaper or an out-of-date price list for reading, and a frosted glass panel with a bell push and 'ring for attention' by way of a greeting. Only slightly better than the unfriendly sliding panel is the presence of a totally bored school leaver, who takes an age to look up from her magazine, knitting or nail polish to mutter 'Yes?' in a manner that clearly implies you are an unwelcome interruption.

Other hazards are the sales office who have no knowledge of something their company is advertising extensively, the complaints department who see their role as conducting a war of attrition against customers and the technical department whose technology apparently stops at the level of a screwdriver.

Have a nice day

This whole area is perhaps most important in the service industries, an area where many companies have made valiant attempts to upgrade service, albeit with varying degrees of success. These include banks, whose little lapses can still include paying a standing order daily instead of monthly or issuing you with plastic cards with which their electronic machines refuse to communicate (it was a bank's computer expert who defined 'user-friendly' as 'very, very complicated but not as complicated as next year's model'); building societies, who think they are banks and want you to vote for them; airlines, who sometimes have their heads in the clouds about service – along with their aeroplanes – and hotels.

To be fair such service businesses are infinitely vulnerable, for example with hundreds of people in a big hotel 24 hours a day the chances of something going wrong for someone are manifold. But it all comes down to people in the end. A year or two ago a story went the rounds about one of the large hotel groups. One of their own senior executives was staying in their flagship London hotel. The service was poor, and finally, at breakfast, he could stand it no longer. He told the waitress who he was, explaining that there were three things she had to offer every customer at breakfast: good food, a nice smile and a few kind words. She listened, took his order and returned a little later with a plate of scrambled eggs and bacon. He looked at her, and after a pause, was rewarded with a slight smile. 'That's better' he said 'and a few kind words?' 'I recommend you don't eat the eggs' came the reply. There is always one, even in the best run organization, but good, consistent customer care and the service standards that result are well worth while.

Without thought and planning this is an area of activity that can become fast and furious. Marketers have to act fast to prevent customers becoming furious.

NOTICE IN SHOP

WARNING – Customers are Perishable

5

Distribution

To market, to market

Distribution is a vital element of marketing. Goods sometimes take a lengthy route from maker to user as they go down what is called the *chain of distribution*. So much so that travelling, rather than arriving at an ultimate consumer, can become an end in itself. Distribution must be treated as one of the variables in business, marketers must choose how to get goods to market rather than simply perpetuating current methods.

There are a host of distributive methods, and middlemen like wholesalers, distributors and agents. The latter all want their percentage – hence the expression 'I can get it for you wholesale' – so the first choice to review is direct selling. This works well for some – cosmetics, double glazing, encyclopedias – but does not enjoy the best image.

But door to door does not in any case suit every business, so consider mail order. This is usually done with, or rather from, a catalogue. The cleverest catalogue producers get the customers to pay for them, make more money from offering credit terms but some then spoil it all by taking weeks and weeks to deliver.

> The grocer sells me addled eggs, the tailor sells me shoddy,
> I'm only a consumer, and I am not anybody.
>
> Nixon Waterman

Another method is party plan, coffee mornings held in customers' homes at which products are displayed and sold. It is best known for the sale of plastic kitchenware, but is also successfully used for children's books, lingerie and more besides.

It is all a question of what suits best. If you elect to go through middlemen, then selling, promotion, indeed the full range of marketing techniques need to be deployed at every stage. Distributors have to be persuaded to stock your product, and persuaded to persuade those who come to them for supplies to buy it. And so on down the chain, up to and including the final consumer.

The same manufacturer may be involved, necessarily, in using a number of routes simultaneously. Tyres for example are sold by the tyre manufacturers to the car manufacturers who fit them to new cars which they sell. They also sell tyres to wholesalers who supply garages, and direct to other garages or tyre centres who are in the replacement market. Also, apparently, to specialist distributors who shred them and display them all over the country alongside motorways.

Sometimes new methods begin to creep in and, before anyone realizes quite what is happening, one such method is no longer new but ubiquitous. Such has happened in the financial services industry with *direct dealing*. Postal and telephone accounts are now the norm. They succeed because they relate to customers' real needs for time saving and convenience. Just lift the telephone at any time of the day or night and there on the other end is good service personified. Well for the most part they have set high standards and this has in turn won customers' confidence and encouraged word-of-mouth promotion. So, now we arrange pensions, insure the house or the car, cancel a direct debit or check our meagre balance by telephone as if it was the most normal thing in the world. And so it is. From the point of view of, say a bank, this method saves money (on staff and branches), allows the creation of a new image and produces loyalty in customers who approve the level and nature of this kind of service. This kind of thing gets very complicated and marketers can profitably spend time drawing *market maps*, a device literally to show where you are going, and help review the distribution options.

Trains, boats and planes

Physical distribution on the other hand is, as the term suggests, concerned with the job of actually shifting goods from one place to another. Warehouses and fork lift trucks (fancy having a special vehicle just to move cutlery). This is an area of considerable cost, and therefore worth considerable effort to organize for maximum efficiency. So remember, next time you are moving slowly round the M25 behind a 16 wheel juggernaut full of plastic toothpicks, it is ultimately the customer's fault.

All wrapped up

Years ago if you wanted to buy, say, a pennyworth of bull's-eyes they were tipped out of a jar. Now they come in quarter pounds wrapped in cellophane, packed into a multicoloured cardboard box which in turn, if you buy one, is put in a paper bag.

Packaging is difficult to get right. At best it may become an integral part of the product and its image, like the ubiquitous Coke bottle. It may also have to do other, different, things, some of them in conflict. It may have to keep a product fresh, safe, or clean. Even as simple a function as this can be misunderstood as one customer discovered in a bookshop saying 'I suppose these copies are cellophane wrapped to keep the dirt out' and receiving the response 'No, Madam, to keep the dirt in.' Packaging has to display information of all sorts and on, say, food products 'E' numbers, health warnings, calorie content and cooking instructions. It has to protect the product *en route* to the customer, it may need to stack conveniently and be more eye catching than its competitors. None of this is any comfort as you reach for the sticking plaster having cut a finger at the end of a twenty minute struggle to get into the wretched thing, only to discover you cannot unwrap that either. Being easy to open seems to rank lower than other criteria, particularly that of persuading customers to buy more. A recent trend is towards quantity, customers are assumed never to want one, or even two or three of anything. Two six-inch nails, one battery or can of beer are all things of the past. It is probably only a matter of time before everything from shoes to sealing wax comes in six-packs.

Something in store

For consumer products of course, unless a more direct route is used, however long the chain it tends to end with some sort of shop, store or retail outlet.

These come in many varieties from the kiosk to the open all hours corner shop, from multiples with many branches to hypermarkets and out of town shopping centres.

You can choose to sell to them all. Or just to deal with some:

- *blanket coverage* means your product will be seen everywhere, and provided you back this with advertising and sales support it should sell well.

- *exclusive distribution* means adopting a more elitist approach, this can work too if the retailers you pick support you. However, 'Only available from authorized stockists' may mean it is genuinely exclusive or that very few shops will agree to stock it.

A good trick is to go for what is called *mass exclusivity*: a product is in fact widely available, but everyone thinks they are one of the few who are on to something special. All the most successful restaurants, for example, have something of this quality.

Whatever retailers you elect to stock your product, they need persuading that they should do so. This necessitates that the contact you organize with them must be regular and persuasive. Several approaches are possible, as outlined below.

Sales representatives

These are your ambassadors out in the field in all weathers; going from shop to shop to sell-in your product.

Merchandisers

These may work with representatives and help the stores display the product effectively. Often this means obtaining space for promotional material, not an easy job as not every supermarket manager welcomes your dumpbin of free footballs. He can imagine what his younger customers will do with them.

Telephone selling

This has, due largely to the increasing cost of representation, become very popular in recent years. Some companies take 80 per cent to 90 per cent of their orders by phone, with calls made to a regular cycle. Indeed some buyers prefer to fantasize about the lovely young girl who telephones so seductively rather than see the salesman. Of course, if they meet, perhaps at a customer party, they may well be sadly disillusioned!

You can use one, or more of these methods or all three together. Your decision will depend, not least, on what is best for the retailer. Retailers are powerful people. If the right ones will not stock your product your chances of marketing success decline. The wise marketer therefore treats his retailers and their buyers very, very carefully.

However you decide to liaise with the stores your products will sell from, once they are in stock, however well your advertising pulls people into the shop, however persuasive your promotion, you are in their hands.

Putting on a show

Retailers want to sell your product. After all they make their living from it. They employ enormous sophistication to do so, and stores are planned and arranged to encourage purchase – to merchandise – in ways that can be scientific, sneaky or both. For example, commodity items like bread and sugar are at the back of the shop, so customers pass by and are tempted by everything else *en route* to them. Children's sweets are at the checkout, where the kids can grab them while you stand in the queue. Best-selling lines are at just the right height to catch the customer's eye, while background music lulls people into a buying mood and the smell of new baked bread wafts through the air (not from the bread but from a machine behind the scenes).

To check how customers react stores use *tachistoscopes*, a device which measures the rate at which customers blink as they look along the shelves. More blinks mean more interest, or dust in the eye. In self-service stores they even have trolleys whose wheels are fixed to aim round and round the shelves when anyone tries to push them to the checkout, an idea they stole from the British Airports Authority whose luggage trolleys all make, crablike, for the red customs channel when you want green, and the taxi line when you want the underground or the bus.

All these techniques have the generic name merchandising. Whatever you call it, 'establishing point-of-sale contact with your consumers' or 'maximizing impulse purchases', means filling the shops and plastering shop windows with masses of gaudy signs. As a good marketer however, you cannot afford to overlook merchandising, so throw good taste to the winds and remember that yellows and reds stand out best in the supermarket situation, especially if they are in fluorescent inks.

Help the retailers with their merchandising, even providing *shelf-talkers* (the nasty cardboard or plastic bits often printed in those fluorescent yellow or red inks and placed close by your product in the self-service store or supermarket to draw the customers' eyes) free, and your products will sell out faster from their stores.

Perhaps nothing illustrates the malleability of consumers more than this kind of in-store activity. Play *Waltzing Matilda* next to the drinks section and people will buy more Australian wines (or French if you choose appropriately evocative music). Really, I do not have to make this up, research in more than one supermarket clearly showed this to be true. Put some rotten fruit by the disinfectants and customers may wrinkle their noses but you will sell more disinfectants. Sorry, I did make that up; but it would not surprise me one bit.

Extreme measures

In recent times attempts to investigate the psychology of customer behaviour have reached almost bizarre heights. The 'science' of *shopper watching* – which uses hidden cameras and microphones in stores, and even has researchers spending entire days with families recording everything to do with their use of supermarket-type products – has become quite extensive. The room in-store where recordings are received and analysed is the *shopping laboratory*. Some weird, but useful, findings are being utilized. For instance, customers react to mass colour. Twenty items in red packs displayed together will sell in greater quantitiy than when they are spread around the store. Why? Who knows? The most extreme form of research in this area is *garbology*: checking shopping habits from an examination of people's dustbins; I kid you not.

> I am the world's worst salesman: therefore I must make it easy for people to buy.
>
> F W Woolworth

Can I help you?

On the one hand retailers use every trick in the book to sell products, on the other hand they can destroy your products' chances of success. Retailers are the schizophrenics of the marketing world. How so?

What about the person behind the counter? Here prevailing standards of service, never mind selling, are often low. Shoppers may be forgiven for assuming that the average shop assistant's main skill lies in holding a conversation with a colleague and looking fixedly away from potential customers simultaneously. The customers often form the strong impression that they are little more than an interruption to the assistant's cosy existence. When they want help it is not there and so when there are sales opportunities they are often missed. The ubiquitous 'Can I help you?', when in any case what is meant is 'May I help you?' is, for the sales assistant, the worst possible start. It does not prompt a conversation; most of us just say 'No, thank you,' or 'I am just looking'. Some are more abrupt. When the customer knows what he wants he is too often told 'There is no demand for that' – when he is standing there asking for it. When he wants advice he is too often confused; asking in the electrical department which of two cassette radios is best, he is told 'This has a graphic equalizer.' A what? And more to the point what does it do? Of course there are exceptions: the assistant who genuinely creates interest, finds out what customers really want and offers what is often referred to as old fashioned service will always succeed.

Sometimes attempts to make life easier for the shopper can backfire. Bar codes, the row of black stripes on packaging and product alike, have been introduced to improve efficiency. They help stock control and they prompt the shop to reorder so that they do not run out of anything. They also allow the cashier to ring up the till so fast customers cannot keep up and it is those struggling to pack up their purchases that hold up the queue. Retailers can certainly be a weak link. The wise marketer will spend some of his time, energy and budget helping the retailer sell his products. Or he runs the shops himself.

Export or die

The British (and perhaps certain other nationalities too) are apt to be a little insular in outlook. Of course there are exceptions, some 90 per cent of the UK's exports are sold by a handful of companies who clearly take a broader view, but the vast majority regard the market as that area firmly within our coastline. For overseas read off limits.

The real trouble is that it is a great big world out there with competitors of every sort and the people in those overseas markets do not always want what we happen to make. Which may be inconvenient, but is exactly what marketing is all about (as you will know if you started reading at the beginning, customers' needs come first).

So the first rule of export marketing is go there. Find out what they want, how they buy it, what flavour it should be or whatever. The second rule is the same, go there. Having found out what is needed tell them you can supply it, competitively and reliably. And the third rule is, surprise, surprise, go there. Deliver. Send your product, back it up with good service, appoint local agents and above all keep in touch.

Of course it can be hard. Hard on the wallet, metabolism, stomach and home life. And no one understands. As the export manager staggers into the office, straight from Heathrow off a long haul flight, tanned only from standing in the sun for four hours at Kuwait airport, his boss looks up briefly and says 'Have a nice time?' Sometimes such a boss is in fact himself involved in the export drive, scheduling an annual sales drive in Florida and two, week-end, visits to Paris as he insists 'No, no, you handle the Lagos deal, George, I wouldn't want to interfere.'

Any chance of achieving international success means not just going there, but ensuring that the product is exactly right for each and every territory in which it is sold. Cars have to comply with the local safety regulations in whatever country they are sold, and there needs to be someone on hand locally to service them once they have been bought. More than one of the big confectionery companies sells chocolate worldwide, but the formula and flavour varies around the world to cater for every local taste. There are so many different ways to be a chocoholic.

All this product variance may well take some organizing, but there are worthwhile markets to be tapped around the world.

So, international business is attractive. For many companies a significant percentage of sales are overseas, or their activities are truly multinational. Just as well too, the country needs the dollars, and francs and yen, and besides think of those marketing everything from safari suits to diarrhoea tablets to export salesmen, they need their market too.

Services too can be exported. The author constitutes what is called an *invisible export* on occasions, travelling overseas to conduct training courses. Services must be delivered, of course, so a wealth of ways exists to set up overseas arrangements. Whatever is sold and wherever it may be sold, the world constitutes a larger market than just home base. Many products that appear everywhere courtesy of the multinationals involve export in the sense of shipping products around as well as international business that may involve many combinations of local manufacture or supply.

Abroad is unutterably bloody and foreigners are fiends.

Nancy Mitford

The last time Britain went into Europe with any degree of success was on 6 June 1944.

Daily Express

Who sold you this then?

The marketer's job is not finished once the product has been sold. The chain of distribution goes full circle and the customer may require after-sales service; either because the product needs regular maintenance, or because something is wrong. Regular maintenance needs to be efficiently organized. Taking three days off work to wait for a plumber who does not call as arranged, and does not even apologize when he finally does, is not likely to make customers keen to do business with the same organization again. Additionally, after-sales service becomes the process for putting right things which should have been right before the product left the factory, but were not. The fact that this costs a company money and reduces profit seems not to prevent a high incidence of such faults. Others make a financial virtue of the situation and charge for putting things right through long-term service contracts.

Memory of customer care at the point of purchase will, whether good or bad, fade in time. Memory of ongoing service, as with a product like a car, is very much part of the body of opinion that influences the next purchase and recommendations before that too. Ensuring that customers' experience and memories are good is a worthwhile part of overall marketing strategy.

While much has been made of planned obsolescence, and some products certainly give every impression of being designed to fall to bits at the earliest possible moment, ultimately even good products do wear out. And replacement bits are big business. Whether it is a washer for the tap, a heel for a shoe, a gasket for the car or a new jet engine for a jumbo, all have to be sold and a great deal of money is spent on them. One ploy is to make and sell the product at a break-even figure, or little margin, the profit coming later on the replacement parts. There are even manufacturers who have designed products that are nothing but bits, children's building systems and certain kinds of knock-down furniture come to mind, some of which are never put together.

Of course, certain companies do work at gaining and succeed in winning a reputation for reliability which can give them a well deserved edge in the market. Though even a lifetime guarantee will only produce such an edge in a worthwhile way if it is unique (and if the product is bought by a sufficiently young market segment to see it as an advantage). If all the competitors in a field do the same the impact is less.

Others find that a reputation for unreliability is difficult to change. Customers' memories are long and linger long after the product or service has changed for the better, this may even be the case when the manufacture is not at fault. It will be a long time before 'Titanic II' is a good name for an ocean liner.

6

'Electronic' marketing

Where did you get this book? (And if you borrowed it, give it back at once and buy your own!) Customers used to buy books, like so much else, from a 'shop'. Now that shop might effectively be in your living room: if you logged onto Amazon and went electronic shopping to buy this, then you are a participant in a revolution. Watch out – this is but one simple example: we all are living in revolutionary times. Everyone is aware of the information technology revolution and the changes to the world that can be laid at its door are legion. One is that this chapter is out of date. The pace of change means that by the time it has got into print, and you read it, things will have moved on. No matter: at least within a reasonable time frame what is most important here are the trends, and the attitude to information technology that is taken with regard to the marketing process.

Better, faster, different

Some general points first. The pace of technological change is frantic. Even considering the longer term, things move fast. Computers have revolutionized the office environment, but not everything has progressed as predicted. Consider the following:

■ Computers themselves have perhaps evolved faster than initial predictions, but what for instance has happened to the much-predicted 'paperless office'? For goodness sake, most people's desks seem as submerged as ever (and some of it is computer printout!).

■ Computers make things more efficient and do things faster, but how long does it take to get to grips with the latest feature and why have such phrases as '*sorry, it's in the computer*' become the ultimate excuse for delay?

■ Computers have reduced costs, but what about the cost of the equipment and the training and the peripherals?

These, and no doubt other statements that could be made and questioned, expose two sides of the proverbial coin. There is truth in both aspects of them. It is too simplistic to expect to say, '*computers make things better*' and expect there to be no downsides. The point about change remains. It took some years for computers to become established in every office, and proportionately less for them to proliferate onto every desk, so that now most executives take it as read that they will type a good deal, perhaps all, of their written output (and if you think that is a chore, try writing a book!). It took even less time from the introduction of e-mail to the point where you are not seen as a serious player without it – *200 messages a day? That's nothing!* New things may well consume us all even more quickly. We will see.

At the same time the sheer pace of change does make problems. The cost of re-equipping or updating equipment, the training – formal or informal, it all takes time and costs money – and such seems to continue in an endless cycle. A new development may be real and useful, but to many people it sometimes seems to last about five minutes. The little ditty below summarizes the feelings of many people as they are faced with the next new gizmo:

I bought a new computer
It came completely loaded
It was guaranteed for 90 days
But in 30 was outmoded.

Though maybe such sentiments are only possible because of the computer industry's marketing success.

There is a saying that *prediction is easy, it's getting it right that's the problem.* With technology, the biggest problem is perhaps the sheer unpredictability of it all; the job of trying to anticipate what will stick and what will not and when things will happen is fraught with difficulty. Yet some marketing success goes to those who get it right.

640K ought to be enough for anyone.

Bill Gates (1981)

Impact across the board

So far, examples may seem to have been primarily in the area of office administration, but the electronic revolution has wider impact. In terms of marketing, there are effects on products and services, and on methods.

Products

The evidence for electronically influenced products is all around us. This includes things that are obviously electronic, such as computers, computer games, digital cameras and personal organizers. It also includes things that appear just electric, such as washing machines and photocopiers, and others such as cars – all of which are overflowing with microchips – and more. More products in the future will be in these general categories; and more again will be gadgets unheard of currently (see box).

The whole process of product development in these circumstances becomes very different to the development of simpler things. Original development may:

- take longer;

- cost more;

- be more complex (and thus more likely to be problematical);

- be more vulnerable to competition.

We can all think of examples of the last. Fax machines saw off telex in a moment. E-mail has largely replaced fax messages (less special fax paper sold, more normal paper as e-mail messages are printed out), audio cassettes were largely sent on their way by compact disks, and a variety of music and video formats currently vie with each other to be the next 'standard'. This kind of dance is typical of many fields from software to toys; only the timescale varies. Updating may follow very quickly. In some product areas new versions follow each other almost on a monthly basis.

GADGETS GALORE

We live in a silicon world, chips are everywhere, the word electronic has become a prefix for almost everything, most of which is described by its initials. There is a new gadget every five minutes and seemingly life would be impossible without them. I am no technophile (well, mostly not), yet some gadgets appeal to me very much indeed.

Imagine this: something that can provide entertainment or information, and do so in sequence or at random (perhaps with an indexing facility). Something that can show you pictures as well as words, yet is small enough to slip in your jacket pocket. That weighs less than a pound and that needs no plugs or adapters – indeed, no external power source. That needs no complex instructions or users' manual and that can be passed around, reused and that will stand up to the wear and tear of its owner's busy life. Imagine also something that can be purchased in any halfway decent shopping centre and on the Internet and that costs around the price of a music CD – sounds like a neat idea?

It certainly is. What is it? It is called a book.

Changing methods

The way things work is being changed by technology. Right across the business world, the range of change is enormous. Think of the role that electronic money transfer and 'hole-in-the-wall' cash machines have played in changing bank branch structure and organization (and remember bank *managers*?). Think too of the developing impact of Internet banking and where that may take us. Such things constitute big changes, and such an example barely scratches the surface of what is going on.

Things change everywhere. Customers used to go into a shop, select goods, pay and that was the end of it. Paying now involves electronic machines at the cash points. These do not just facilitate the taking of money (and make it possible to employ staff who cannot add up!); they are the tip of an electronic iceberg of integrated computer systems. The cash point registers the sale, communicates with stock control and more supplies of a product can be ordered automatically when stocks decline to a certain level. If a customer uses a card (increasingly so-called 'smart' cards), whether a credit card or one linked to a loyalty scheme, then the sale can be recorded against an individual. Buy product X and the customer suddenly starts to receive promotions through the post for product X or its competitors (something like a supermarket can charge their suppliers to send this sort of material on their behalf). Such schemes can be linked back to the cash point, so that offer coupons are distributed to particular customers in a way that reflects their buying record – and also, of course, in a way intended to influence their future buying.

Marketing has seen to it that there is no such thing as a simple purchase these days.

> I have yet to see any problem, however complicated, which when looked at in the right way, did not become still more complicated
>
> Poul Anderson

Again space prohibits a lengthy list of examples, but the current complexity and future possibilities are clear. For any particular organization there are matters here that must be coped with. For example, a supermarket might be more resistant to seeing salespeople if their computer system is able to reorder directly. Such salespeople then have to find new ways of prompting the discussions they want, discussions that go a long way beyond reordering and which involve promotion, display and much else, all of which are vital to the marketing effort.

As well as difficulties there are also opportunities, areas where you can choose to get involved, despite greater complexity, if you see an advantage. For example, a search of what is new and an assessment of how it might help has become a prerequisite part of marketing thinking. Examples may well date, but the following show what is now possible – indeed, what is now normal in terms of going about things:

- Computers can now calculate optimum merchandising arrangements. A company making a range of products different in size, price, margin and rate of turnover can work out what mix of product selection should be put on any particular amount of shelving that a store allocates to their brand, at the touch of a button. No spare space is then left on the shelf and turnover and profit generation are maximized.

■ Field sales staff now routinely carry computers and can use them, for instance, to give an instant answer to customer questions about stock and delivery of a product.

■ Customer details can be accessed instantly during transactions just by the mention of, say, a postcode; this facilitates many processes, for example dealing at a distance from a call centre.

Computer and other IT developments will doubtless produce many more developments of this sort, all either actively assisting marketing effort, or with which marketing must fit in if it is to retain credibility.

In addition, this revolution has spawned a whole new dimension to marketing, putting a letter 'e' in front of everything from commerce to retailing.

> Any company, old or new, that does not see this technology as important as breathing could be on its last breath.
>
> Jack Welsh

Electronic marketing

This whole area, one certainly subject to continuing change and development, involves the Internet at its heart: it is this that has allowed the birth of e-commerce in all its forms. Such things tend to be spoken of as if they were something new. In fact, though *how* they operate is clearly new, their role and effect are simply to add to the choice of methodology available, particularly in two different areas: promotion and distribution. Let us take these in turn:

Promotion

Web sites, for all their technical wizardry, are only another method of communicating with customers (and sometimes – see distribution below – of doing business: e-tailing). Consider Web sites, first and foremost, as a promotional channel. As such they must command attention, put over their message clearly and act to persuade. They must also be convenient and easy to use. At this stage, and for a while yet, this means appealing to people, in part at least, who see themselves to be other than at the forefront of computer literacy. (See box *help please*.) A Web site may be an electronic alternative to many things: a brochure, a salesperson, a showroom or shop window, a magazine and more (in any combination).

Retailing and distribution

Here we are in the territory of what has become known as *e-commerce*. This is a situation where the whole business transaction, or most of it, takes place over the airwaves, as one might say. The point about clarity and convenience made above is perhaps even more important here. Some things are up and running and working well. Customers like them. They may conduct their banking and finances through Internet accounts, they may order many different things, computers, pizzas, books and CDs, and much more, from Internet sites. But one point about this that will be worth watching is the relationship between Internet shopping and conventional retailing.

Some things can work fine exclusively through Internet channels. If someone wants to buy a new novel by a favourite author, they are probably happy not even to look at it – they tap into *amazon.com* or whoever, call up the title and place their order (with maybe a little price comparison along the way). Other purchases are more complex. If someone wants a new CD player, say, they may well want to look at it – better still hear it – and check it out first. They go to a retailer and do just that. Then later they might elect to visit a number of sites on the Internet, compare prices, check delivery and so on and place an order. What many people will not do is simply order a machine seen only on a monitor screen.

In other words, a broad retail sector is currently necessary for certain kinds of e-commerce to work. E-tailing has a parasitic relationship with its traditional counterpart. How this works out and what future buying practice will be like is still uncertain. That said, e-commerce works well for many things, the fields in which it operates are growing and more and more people are either experimenting with this sort of shopping or expressing confidence in it by regular use. Current predictions for the farther future include the demise of supermarkets. All bulk goods, from tissues to cat food, will be ordered online and delivered. Customers will only visit stores for things that demand real choice or checking; as a result stores will be smaller, but departments such as the bakery or cheese counter will expand. Again, we will see.

HELP PLEASE

An important fact about the nature of Web sites is worth emphasizing:

They must be customer focused.

This may seem obvious. But it also means that they should *not* necessarily:

- incorporate everything that is technologically possible (perhaps just because someone regards doing so as a challenge);

- be comprehensive (some things that might be incorporated are surely more important than others);

- be interactive in every possible way (though there may be strong reasons for having an interactive element);

- incorporate every technological gizmo known (some sites will aim for customers who are themselves more technically sophisticated or demanding, others must recognize that not everyone is of this persuasion – at least not yet).

It does mean that the objectives that give a Web site its *raison d'être* should be customer orientated – it should be designed to work in the way *they* want, or at least find they like; and to do so without any great gaps in its capability.

An example will illustrate the point. One evening I contacted two Web sites. One was *amazon.com*, the American bookseller (they, of course, sell more than books but it was a book order that prompted the contact). The site is especially clear and easy to use. All was going well, a few interesting minutes were spent checking out soon-to-be-published books in favourite areas and an order was placed. Then a problem materialized (about credit cards – the details do not matter). The system did not cope with this, and the user's understanding did not cope with how to deal with it either. In a shop, of course, you would just ask. Same here – a message was sent, by e-mail, and a prompt reply spelt out clearly exactly what needed to be done. No problem. When a site works this well people will return (even those who do not see themselves as at the forefront of things electronic).

The same evening another site was contacted. It was a nightmare of insufficient information and confusion (it would be unkind to name them), and after some minutes of struggle, frustration and travelling in electronic circles any attempt to do business with its owner was abandoned.

The difference was very obvious with two contrasting sites seen alongside each other. Why should one be so good, and another so poor? After all the technology is there, some people make it work and get their customers saying, *'This is good,'* whatever the technical sophistication of the site. Even a simple site is often able to do a good job and to make customers feel it is good. It is probably in the approach. Maybe the second site mentioned above had been set up too quickly. Maybe it had been created on the assumption that customers are clairvoyant, or maybe the objectives for the site were unclear.

Whatever the reason, the point here is clear. Doing business in this way makes for exposure; no order materialized in this example. Assuming people contact a site at all, they will notice how it works (not least compared with others), they will talk about it to others and they will elect to come back – or not, as the case may be. Image is affected; so are future business prospects. Going about the set-up process needs care and consideration, and it to this we turn next.

Going electronic

A complete rundown on every method of marketing that incorporates the Internet is beyond our brief here. However, some comment
about the set-up and role of a Web site follow, both as practical
advice in its own right, and as an example of the thinking and
approaches that need to be applied in this area.

The job of setting up a Web site can be time-consuming and expensive. So too can be maintaining it and keeping it up to date.

Some organizations acted very early as technology created this
opportunity. Others however, judging by what was created, acted
solely because it was flavour of the month, *something that had to be
done,'* perhaps to keep up with competitors, perhaps to pander to
the ego of someone involved and enthusiastic. Whatever the
reasons, there are certainly examples where such early action was
ill considered (or indeed not considered at all), and where time and
money were spent to no good effect. Such an initiative needs
thinking through; the first question is very obvious and straightforward.

> If (technology) keeps up, man will atrophy all his limbs but the push-
> button finger.
>
> Frank Lloyd Wright

What are the objectives for the Web site?

It is not suggested that there will be only one. Several are likely, but
they all need to be spelt out and to be specific. Ultimately it will be
important to know whether the cost of the set-up is delivering what
was intended; and this is important to how a site is developed. Two
particular purposes predominate. A Web site may be intended as:

■ **a reference point**: Perhaps the site is in part a source of reference. It is designed for people to consult it to obtain information (and be impressed by it at the same time). For example, many accountancy firms have sites on which you can check current tax information or rates. Such may save time and effort otherwise expended in other ways. Perhaps it is intended that a site will play a more integral part in the overall sales and marketing process. In that case, it is sensible to measure its effectiveness in terms of counting the number of new contacts it produces and, in turn, how many of those are, in due course, turned into actual paying customers.

Note: Any Web site should be checked to see whether good feedback results from its use and to examine the specific results it brings (for example, counting new contacts or revenue coming from new contacts). Similarly, when a site is initially being set up, marketing people must ensure consideration of this is an inherent part of the process.

■ **an ordering point**: In addition, a site may be designed so that people can order and pay for products through direct contact with it. For example, a consultant might offer a survey of some sort, primarily to put an example of their expertise and style in the hands of prospective clients (though doing so might also be a source of revenue). A product company might, of course, have their whole range listed and available to order off the site. In this case, not only must the ordering system work well, and this means it must be quick and easy to navigate for whoever is doing the ordering, but the follow-up must be good too. Any initial good impression given will quickly evaporate if whatever is ordered takes forever to arrive or needs several chasers. One hazard to good service is to demand too much information as an order is placed. Some facts are key and, of course, this kind of contact represents an opportunity to create a useful database; but turning ordering into an experience reminiscent of the Spanish Inquisition will hardly endear you to people. If the site is that of an e-tailer, then the range of what is sold may be wider than that of competitors, yet it must always impress with its ease of operation.

Three distinct tasks

With clear objectives set, there are then three distinct marketing tasks to be addressed. These are:

1. **to attract people to the site**: the mere existence of the site set-up does not in itself mean people will log onto it in droves, much less that the specific type of people you want to do so will act in this way. Other aspects of wider promotion must draw attention to it and this may vary from simply having the Web site address on your letterhead to incorporating mention (and perhaps demonstration) of it into a range of promotional methods from advertisements to brochures. Simple, cost-effective methodology may work well here, with just a simple promotional postcard acting to prompt people (customers or others) to investigate the site.

2. **to impress people when they see it**: both with its content and by its presentation. This means keeping a close eye on customers' views and accommodating all the necessary practicalities as it is set up. For example, all sorts of impressive graphics are possible. They can look creative and may well act to inform and impress. Certainly there should be some. But such devices can take a long time to download and, if that is what people are being encouraged to do, they may find this tedious (at worst curtailing their contact because of its time-consuming nature). This is more likely if the graphics seem more like window dressing than something that enhances the content in a way that is genuinely necessary or useful to customers.

3. **to encourage repeat use**: this may or may not be one of the objectives. If it is, then efforts have to be made to encourage re-contacting (again using a whole range of prompts) and this too may involve an overlap with other forms of communication.

In addition to the points made above, other factors also need to be considered carefully:

■ **site content**: what should be presented (this is an ongoing job, not a one-off);

■ **interaction**: how contacting the Web site can prompt a dialogue;

■ **topicality**: how up to date it should be (this affects how regularly it needs revision, from daily to annually);

■ **ease of use**: its convenience and accessibility (does it have a suitable navigation mechanism?);

■ **image**: will it look consistent (and not as if it has been put together, like the proverbial horse that ended up as a camel, by committee);

■ **security**: the protection it needs (is anything confidential, is it vulnerable to hackers, etc and will customers feel their own information is safe?).

Overall, setting up and using a Web site will need the same planning, co-ordination and careful execution as any other form of marketing communication. In addition, it is likely to necessitate active, ongoing co-operation from numbers of people around the organization who will provide and update information. This may be a larger job than it appears at first sight, not just because of the numbers of individuals and departments involved, but because they may have differing perspectives (with, say, research and marketing differing about the depth of technical information that should be included). This aspect can present quite a challenge, especially in an organization of any size. Clearly, responsibility for the site and what it contains must be unequivocally laid at someone's door, together with the appropriate authority to see it through. Another challenge may be to get computer and marketing people to work effectively together. Marketing must, for instance, ensure that computer staff understand the objectives and do not proceed on the basis of including everything that is technically possible or fun to do.

> You probably knew a geek in high school or college. You remember, the one with the thick glasses and the silly laugh. Now, thanks to the computer revolution, many geeks make 10 times as much money as you do.
>
> Laurence A Canter and Martha S Siegel

At the same time, someone does need to have the knowledge that is necessary from a technical standpoint. This may be internal or external, but it needs to be linked to an understanding of marketing and/or the ability to accept a clear brief if an appropriate scheme is to be created. There is a real danger of simply applying all the available technology, building in every bell and whistle, simply because it is possible. Practical solutions are necessary to meet clear objectives (and these should always be customer-focused).

If a site is to be useful, that is if it is to comprise an effective part of the marketing mix, then sufficient time and effort must be put in to get it right. And the ongoing job of maintaining it must be borne in mind from the beginning.

Ever more possibilities (and complications)

Among the changes technology is bringing are numbers of things that can act to make electronic marketing work better, though they also make the job of the marketing person more difficult – just how complex do they consider it is worth getting?

Linking in research

One interesting and practical development is the recent availability of standard, cost-effective software packages that can work as an integral part of a Web site and monitor how it is used. In fact, there are now such add-ons that are better described as research tools: they allow regular research and formal monthly analysis about exactly who is using a Web site, their precise characteristics, and how and why they are in touch with the site. It will not be long before they can identify the eye colour and inside leg measurement of someone who logs onto the site!

The intention is specifically to obtain information that will make the Web site a more accurate and effective marketing tool; increasingly such packages can be tailored to the requirements of an individual organization.

Linking to sales

Similarly, there are now systems that allow a visitor to a Web site to click on an icon that instigates their receiving a telephone call to discuss some specific detail of an offer. This can be instant and on-line, so that both parties can look at the site on screen and discuss it. Alternatively, a call can be made some time later. It depends on the system. Such a contact is, of course, essentially a sales one. If it is made sufficiently easy, then it will generate conversations that can influence the likelihood of sales that might otherwise never occur.

Utilizing appropriate technology

Some applications are particularly well suited to a specific product or service. For example, it is possible to book a hotel following a detailed inspection of it over the Internet. Before long customers will do this in a 'virtual' way that is almost as real as walking around the actual building; they may even find one day that if they check a resort hotel, there will be technology that can simulate the feel of sand between their toes! This parallels what many customers want to do. If a real alternative to actually visiting a hotel is provided, something that is judged by its users as better than any sort of paper brochure, then a particular provider will have an edge in the market against their competitors.

It is said that the future is not what it used to be. Certainly marketing people have a whole new area of activity, and new skills as well, to get to grips with. Precisely how it can – and will – affect matters over the next months and years may be uncertain. That it *will* affect us all is not.

> It is the business of the future to be dangerous.
>
> A N Whitehead

> Too many marketers assume that the future will hold back and wait until they're ready for it. It won't.
>
> Faith Popcorn

The interface between marketing and all things IT is here to stay. How marketing reacts to all this must be carefully considered. Just because something is technically possible does not mean that it will work in customer terms, as all those with now worthless shares in *doomedfromthestart.com* will testify. The electronic dimension of marketing is not something that can ever be got 'right', and put on one side as needing no more care and attention. For better or for worse, marketing people are faced with an ongoing process as change continues and new elements of all this come into view. It presents both a challenge and an opportunity, but marketing is inherently about the creative exploitation of opportunities – so watch this space.

Note: If you have read this chapter, then you should know that microscopic chips hidden in the full stops have just recorded your every detail to the publisher's database; you will hear from them soon. Just kidding, but – who knows?

7

The future

Prediction is an uncertain business and perhaps especially foolhardy at the start of a new millennium and in a dynamic field such as marketing. Nevertheless it is worth ending with some thoughts about trends and possibilities for the future (and if anything turns out to be idiotically wrong then the chances are that this book will be out of print before anyone notices). So, first things first – and with marketing that means markets and customers.

Markets

Economies will doubtless continue to go up and down, but if the long term produces growth then consumers will have more money to spend in the future. Social changes will continue to have an impact on this. In recent years, with an increasing number of households having two partners working, there has been more disposable income. But time becomes doubly precious, so spending on convenience foods, say, or a decent holiday when a rest can be taken, become more important. Many older people (the 'Grey' market) now have more disposable income in retirement than they did in the past. Children are already a tangible market in themselves and seem to exert influence over purchases at younger and younger ages; so much so that some marketers would willingly beam their promotion into prams.

There will continue to be such major changes. Some will occur quickly, others will take longer and some will no doubt creep up on us and catch us unawares. Predicting similar changes will bring rewards for those that do it accurately or react quickly. Will women have babies earlier or later in life? (Or will someone successfully market cloning – *Clones R Us* – and will genetic engineering mean all clothing can be sold in one size?). Will increasing environmental concerns (such as noisy jets and spoiled islands) create a downturn in the package holiday industry and a boom in Bournemouth, as holidays at home again become the in thing? Conversely, how long will it be before you can holiday in orbit, or on the moon? Marketing must continue to cater for people by relating to the real way they live, and another sign of this is recent advertising in which single parents, gay couples (or, in due course perhaps, robots) have become as common as the nuclear family of old.

Consumers will themselves be affected by many other changes as time goes by. These may range from government legislation (on product safety for instance) to events seemingly far removed from the commercial arena. Yet a larger hole in the ozone layer will help sell more sun lotion and global warming and rising sea levels may create new markets entirely (with boats outselling cars, perhaps).

Busier consumers, with more experience (and perhaps more guidance from the boom in *Watchdog* style television and radio programmes and publications) will become ever more demanding and fickle. Their loyalty will last about five minutes unless marketers hook them in via loyalty schemes, cards and rewards or put out irresistible ongoing promotions. Customer service will be paramount; even more so than now. Marketing activity is going to have to work harder and harder to keep ahead of ever more sophisticated consumers. And research, despite burgeoning statistical techniques, may find it harder in future to offer reliable advice about what such people will do next.

Today the world

Markets are getting ever more international. The same brands, even the same advertisement or television commercial, appear in Boston, Bombay and Birmingham. This trend will continue, and as more developing countries decide, or are persuaded, that they cannot do without such essentials as fast food and mobile phones the world-wide opportunities will increase. Companies too will continue to grow in size, with mergers creating worldwide conglomerates at once powerful and vulnerable.

Other elements of international change will affect marketing. In Europe goods of all sorts are now being priced in the new Euro currency, but it is early days in this change and how many of us have confidence that politicians can cook up anything so complex and implement it without a hitch? Though any hitches that do occur will no doubt provide an opportunity for someone. That said, the world will no doubt continue to shrink and, not least, to do so by electronic means – already you can order this book as easily from an igloo in Greenland as from anywhere else in the world just by dialling into the Internet. Which brings us naturally to things technical.

Technology rules (regardless)

Technology is developing faster than ever. And new technology of all sorts can change marketing. It does so mainly in three areas: creating new products, new ways of distributing them and directly affecting marketing methods. Some of these issues were invest-igated in the previous chapter, so only brief reference is necessary here.

New products

Not so long ago mobile phones, electronic organizers, bagless vacuum cleaners and digital televisions did not exist. Most people

managed to live reasonably full lives without them – what consumers do not know about they do not miss. And for those still
struggling to get to grips with their video recorder, the whole pace
of change is somewhat daunting. Yet certainly the first three
examples, picked at random from the plethora of new things to
come along in recent years, have been marketing successes. It is
certainly possible for new products to become major players.

Regardless of how some people may feel about it, technology, and
especially so-called IT (Information Technology), develops apace.
Some markets, including computers, are now geared almost entirely
around upgrading and new versions appear almost daily. Who
knows what awaits? Some developments will wreak havoc in
existing markets in the way that fax machines quickly removed telex
from the scene. Others go through lengthy periods of uncertainty,
as video recorders did before a 'standard' format (VHS) emerged the
winner, and as is happening again with new systems for playing
music and film (though another development is systems that allow
music to be downloaded from the Internet track by track. As this
avoids copyright payment, perhaps music will simply cease to be
recorded as there will be no money in it!).

In some areas, years of development and large amounts of money
are invested to produce something like a new jet engine that is
quieter or uses less fuel. Or a pharmaceutical product that sells in
quantity worldwide like Viagra (which strategically must be a
classic case of tapping into a soft market). Simple things can sweep
the board too. Where would we be without the now ubiquitous
'yellow sticky' (the 3M company's 'Post-it' notes)? Developed from
a simple adhesive originally rejected as being too weak to be useful,
these have become an essential in every office and home.

Who knows what will be next? If I could predict that I would not
be writing this, I would be patenting the idea. Products that make
life easier, help the environment or which are simply fun will always
have a good chance of success. Never mind high technology,
personally, I look forward to a milk carton that opens easily and

pours properly and an airline seat that can be sat in by someone other than a dwarf with a growth deficiency.

Distribution

Technology is behind many developments in distribution, for example the whole direct contact financial services business – from telephone banking to insurance – was made possible by, as much as anything, the development of the computer and telephone systems that its operators use.

The main current change that looks significant for the future is the ability to order products and services from a Web site. How far this will go is anyone's guess. Meanwhile simply maximizing the possibilities of existing methods continues to provide success for some, as Pret a Manger did retailing the humble sandwich.

Marketing methods

Here technology is again acting to change how things are done. This is particularly true of retailing. Information gathered about consumers, through electronic checkout equipment, smart cards and so on, is allowing more and more precise marketing activity to be deployed on an individual basis. Customers can now, in some stores, zap the products they select as they walk around the store, arriving at the checkout ready to pay the bill and saving themselves time and the store money. How long will it be before someone who habitually shops on a Thursday gets a telephone call to check what time they will be in the shop (or ask why they have not come)? Already promotions are directed specifically to groups and individuals based on a record of their shopping habits and the brands they favour.

Any change may give marketers new things to cope with, for example:

■ Will more television channels fragment audiences and make directing advertising effectively more difficult?

■ Will technology give consumers a way of 'bleeping out' ads? Already the commercial breaks in the large number of programmes recorded and watched later are routinely skipped.

■ Will the willingness of consumers, increasingly used to telephone or computer contact, to see sales people face to face decline?

Other developments may give rise to new issues altogether. Currently those signing up for a Sky Television Digibox (whatever that is) have to sign agreement to their box being connected by a phone line to a central database. The company can telephone with no audible ring, maybe in the middle of the night, and collect data on viewing habits. A first step perhaps to a barrage of faxed advertisements travelling in the other direction and targeted in light of the data gathered? Maybe people will rebel; we must wait and see. Technology can be a two-edged sword. Sometimes its advantages are obvious; sometimes it makes things more difficult. Perhaps this applies to consumers and marketing people alike.

Taking marketing forward

So how do marketers go about making the future happen as they want?

A creative process

There is an old saying that *good ideas don't care who has them*. A manager is certainly not paid to have all the ideas their work and continuing success make necessary, but they must use their team in an essentially creative way to ensure there are sufficient ideas being produced on an ongoing basis. In marketing, creativity is fundamental. Marketing must not just inform people about products and services and do so persuasively; it must make it easy and satisfying for them to buy. In addition, it must differentiate. Everything must be done in a way that makes an offering seem more desirable, better value and a better course to pursue than that of competitors.

So marketing people must see nothing as fixed: their branding, packaging, advertising and promotion, distribution and all the methods and techniques that they use to help ensure success – everything is ripe for change. Always. And nothing is ruled out. Unfortunately there is a problem. New ideas do not just fall out of the trees like leaves in autumn; they need generating. And even when generated they must prove effective if they are to make a positive difference and the person who thought of them is going to survive within the organization.

Yet the volume of duff ideas shows just how difficult it all is. And this in turn makes it more difficult still. Think about product names. A currently successful brand of spread (what used to be called margarine) is named *I can't believe it's not butter*. Seemingly it works, and – with hindsight – seems like a neat idea. But originally? – I wonder what the reaction was when this was first suggested: an oddball six-word brand name when most of the competition used one – *Get out of here!* You need courage and persuasive powers in marketing, not just the ability to dream up ideas.

> An idea that is not dangerous is unworthy of being called an idea at all.
>
> Oscar Wilde

Other ideas seem, again with hindsight, doomed from the start. Whoever thought that it was a good idea to change the name of PricewaterhouseCooper's consulting operation to '*Monday*', for instance? This is a major accounting firm, people who are paid by others to advise them, for goodness sake. It was, in my humble opinion, ridiculous. What is more it was rapidly seen as such and dropped; but only after a great deal of time, money and work had been put into conceiving and actioning the change. It is perhaps unfair to make fun of such things (though it has to have been the silliest name idea ever, sorry I digress), but it does make the point that such things are difficult to get right.

Two kinds of creativity are worth differentiating:

- *Creating difference:* which implies something fairly radical: a new product, a new name or a new approach;

- *Building on success:* it is a different, and perhaps easier, process to build on something that has an existing success in the market. The *Harry Potter* books perhaps make a good example. The publishers had to spot their potential, publish the first one and get the process started, but once initial success became apparent the process of keeping sales moving forward, while still needing thought, care and creativity, is more straightforward than exploring virgin territory.

Note: Actively working to create, maintain and extend word of mouth publicity has recently been dubbed marketing to generate *ideaviruses*.

Marketing needs both kinds of creativity (even that which includes an element of copying), and the rate at which it needs them deployed is increasing. Once doing well in the market, a good product, backed by good promotion and service, can keep ahead for quite a while. In some businesses the rate at which customers demand change is accelerating and bears no relationship to how things used to be. Someone in one of the major retail fashion chains was quoted recently as saying that the fashion seasons (spring, summer etc.) were effectively dead and that they now needed new stock in the shops 'every two weeks'.

Idea generation

It is important that marketing gives time to creativity. Much of what needs to be done in marketing is routine – designed to keep activity bubbling along and maintain sales continuity. Considering anything novel can be squeezed out by sheer pressure of work, particularly if coming up with new approaches is not easy.

A number of factors about the way marketing is organized help prompt creativity. Working with agencies (advertising, sales promotion and so on) works, in part, because it involves more people and specialist and creative skills. Research helps too, after all it is what potential customers want that matter most, rather than just what someone internally thinks is a neat idea. Research surveys can test ideas and check how customers feel about them. This is not a certain process, and some ideas are implemented largely unchecked, or even in the face of negative feedback, and still prove successful. However sophisticated marketing method becomes there is still room for an element of gut-feel.

In many companies specific opportunities are set up to prompt creative idea generation: regular meetings, brainstorming – anything that will get people to 'think outside the box'. It is important. If it were to be shown that holding planning meetings in a cold store made marketing people more creative, then the sales of fur-lined coats to such people would jump overnight.

> If at first an idea isn't totally absurd, there's no hope for it.
>
> Albert Einstein

No stone unturned

As long as marketing people draw breath there will be new marketing methods to report on. It is rather like an arms race. As one side improves their weapons or changes their tactics, so the other takes action to leapfrog them. This takes various forms and what an individual organization does may be truly inventive or a permutation formed by creative copycatting. For example, in the process of trying to make marketing messages distinctive, smaller and smaller groups (segments and niches) are identified, or contrived, and become discrete targets. Some follow social changes, so it is acceptable now to market to the *pink* (gay) sector or to particular ethnic groups; if a sector responds, it will go on being targeted. Others grow slowly but take on real substance, as has done the sector of people working independently from home, who are a market for a wide range of products and services from stationery and computers to photocopiers and indemnity insurance.

Methods themselves have a life cycle almost like a product. Once upon a time *call centres* were unheard of. Soon, spurred on largely by the developments in banking, they jumped to being everywhere. And they did not just administer things, they sold you things. Then, when many organizations operated them, and many customers had got used to the idea, they expanded further. Their very nature means that they can be anywhere: so people in Bombay are being trained so that they can chat naturally about everyday issues (for example, fish and chips and bus queues), enabling them to talk to customers without it being realized that they are overseas. So if your bank wants to sell you travel insurance when you ask for your foreign currency, and also insists on knowing whether you had a chip butty for tea all in an impenetrable East European accent, then you will at least know what is going on. Now, what many people used to like doing over the telephone, they prefer to do online (for example, banking, again). Mobile phone development is adding more permutations and change will continue, no doubt until 'old fashioned' call centres are dead and gone. Every marketing method changes progressively as it is used and refined in a way that takes account of feedback from customers and reaction from competitors.

If I called a wrong number, then why did you answer the phone?

James Thurber

Whenever one reviewed marketing there would be examples of new methodology. Some of it might exist as a momentary test, quickly disappearing as it is found wanting. Some of it might be hailed as a major innovation, falling into place among the plethora of other tactics in the mix as other, newer or better, ways follow it along. Some may achieve a significant place in the armoury of the marketer – for a while at least.

Few marketing methods are right for every product, service or organization remember. Some things work well in one context, not at all in others. That said, the following give some idea of how the mix is changing:

- **partnership marketing**: there is a growing trend for marketing to involve collaborations – two or more organizations working together in a way that involves co-branding, alliances, joint promotions, joint ventures or sponsorship. Obviously the participants need to be non-competitive, but more than that they need to share a common purpose. An example might be an airline working with a tour operator or a hotel group. An arrangement might be a one-off, transient one or relate to a longer-term alliance. In this way both parties might be able to do things, and access people, in a way that would be impossible, or simply not affordable (cost sharing is one motivation), on their own.

- **re-branding**: this is when a product remains essentially the same but is given a new (brand) name. Sometimes a company may hit trouble and need to change its image, or a brand might be taken over along with the company using the name and the new owner wants to make changes. But essentially re-branding is the term used when it is simply decided that a name change is the best route to future progress (it may not even mean that the brand is in trouble). Of course, everything can change along with the name: so new advertising and perhaps new positioning or a new image is possible. One company that did this is the mobile phone operation that was originally British Telecom's BT Cellnet and which now trades as O2 (what?). A funny name perhaps, but one of their main competitors is *Orange* and that was considered a weird choice by many when it launched, but it has not held it back.

■ **database marketing**: this is a term that encompasses a good deal, but the common factor is the thought of personalizing marketing as much as possible using the vast amount of information it is now possible to collect about customers. A bank sending material to sell insurance, mortgages or investments to existing customers should be able to match pretty well with their actual circumstances. So, if you hobble into your bank every week because you have a wooden leg, they should not mail you about walking holidays. Well, banks do not actually sell holidays (yet), but you get the point – if they personalize and target accurately, on the other hand, then they are probably using database-marketing methods, and these can be more effective than a simple shotgun approach.

■ **churning**: some methods are somewhat weird. Churning – or, more completely, *product churning* – is launching a range of products in the hope that some will do well and the belief that *only* some of them will do well. Thus a company might configure several different holiday packages to a particular country, market the range, but aim to fill more of some than others. Similarly, if you belong to a book club, it is probably one of several slightly differently configured ones (each making different initial offers) all actually run by the same organization.

■ **galimatias marketing**: this is marketing to babies in the womb. Mothers to be are persuaded to play tapes to their 'bump' and the soothing music and soft words ensure that the babies are born with an instinctive liking for certain brand names, growing up to demand the relevant items once they are old enough to be wheeled around the supermarket.

Galimatias marketing? Well, actually not. I made that one up (galimatias means gibberish). But rest assured, if such a thing were possible, someone would no doubt want to do it. Meantime the search for new methods will continue, and new ideas, new permutations of old ones and just ones that have been copied from elsewhere will continue to feature in the growing list of what constitutes the marketing mix.

> Creativity is great, but plagiarism is faster.
>
> Anon

A final point here. I am singling out individual methods, but the mix overall is what matters. Different methods must work in tandem, and all must suit the organization, being compatible with its way of working, its image and its customers. Marketing may ride on the corporate power of an existing image that does much of the organization's marketing for it – think of the long-term positive and powerful image of Marks & Spencer. Or marketing may have to create a powerful image first to make what else it has to do easier (or re-create a powerful image – think again of Marks & Spencer after their decline from favour). Such an example is important: no organization is guaranteed to do good business forever. The mighty can and do tumble on occasion and marketing must assume nothing and work constantly in hostile markets to build and maintain their business.

Desperation

There are evidently businesses where you can make money by sending someone to sit on someone's doorstep for five hours until the householder gives in and talks to them (companies seeking to get customers compensation for accidents, for one). But the effect is short term. I heard of this on a consumer radio programme, and that sort of adverse publicity will, along with common sense and word of mouth, forewarn most future prospects. It is no way to build a long-term business. But. . .

Some organizations are prepared to take a risk, adopting marketing tactics that are, frankly, not as straightforward as they might be; and I am choosing my words carefully here.

One that has already been mentioned is *confusion pricing* (page 25). But there is also a wider-ranging tactic known as *confusion marketing*. Here more radical steps are taken to intentionally confuse consumers and steal a march on competitors. One of the best-known brands in the world, Coca Cola, has sued several companies for marketing drinks in packaging that came too close to their long-developed image. More recently the supermarket Asda launched a chocolate biscuit called *Puffin* in packaging curiously reminiscent of the brand leader *Penguin*. Again legal action, involving the quaint spectacle of lawyers debating the similarities or lack of them of two black and white seabirds, resulted in change. The packaging was redesigned, though the name was allowed to remain. Another case that has been called confusion marketing involved the children's drink *Sunny Delight* which was designed to look like a fruit juice product, the implication being that it was better for health than its contents warrant. Allegedly. Steps were even taken to ensure that its style and packaging meant it was displayed alongside fruit juices in refrigerated display areas.

Now far be it for me to suggest that marketing should be without any sort of guile. It needs to make a strong case and it needs to use any method available. But there is a line to be drawn here. Confusion over such things as product contents (exaggerating the extent to which it is environmentally friendly, say, or safe or healthy) may be covered by legislation. For the rest it should be covered by common sense. Extreme confusion marketing can backfire, and become self-defeating. Consumers resent it, or they notice the legal battles it instigates, and vote with their purses; or rather with a lack of them. On the other hand, it is said that there is no such thing as bad publicity, so perhaps in the long term. . . you decide.

Other marketing methods may have a self-defeating element to them. One currently being debated, amidst demands for legislation, is advertising through e-mail: what is called *spamming* (evidently so-called after the sketch in a *Monty Python* programme where everything in a café came with spam, whether you wanted it or not). Spam defines *unsolicited* messages (supplying regular information to people who have requested it is another matter, and is called *permission marketing*). The very low cost of doing it makes it irresistible to some and, while most people might tolerate a small amount – or even find it useful – the proportion of such material that is pornographic looks set to get some restrictions in place.

Certainly any marketer must balance any upset likely to be done to perhaps the bulk of potential customers, with the benefit of getting through to, and securing orders from, a few. If you want one view, I think spamming is totally counterproductive – *stop it, please.* And I dread to think what will happen when picture texting takes off on mobile phones.

At the end of the day, its recipients must find any activity that becomes part of the marketing process acceptable. Some of it may annoy somewhat (as direct mail seems to do), but the trick is to combine elements that make something both acceptable *and* persuasive into whatever method may be used. What does so will continue to change, and the search to find the mix that works best for any particular organization, product or service will continue as long as there are things to be sold and people to buy them. Ain't marketing wonderful!

One thing that fuels this process of change and extends the ever-burgeoning list of marketing methods is competition. A major part of what marketing people do is designed either to catch up with, or to steal a march on, their competitors. So, everything must be done with a firm eye on the outside world and on competition in particular.

Competition

Of one thing marketing people everywhere can be absolutely sure. Competitiveness is going to increase and more and more of what marketing must do will need to be directed at differentiating an organization from the competition. This factor is perhaps the most important one in terms of its influence on marketing and whether marketing activity can be made successful; it thus makes it an appropriate note on which to move towards an end. It is already insufficient just to have a good product, just to say it is good or even to do so in a creative and persuasive way. Consumers have to be given not only reasons to buy but reasons to buy one product rather than another.

It is how marketers rise to this challenge, orchestrating the whole way marketing works, from product development to after-sales service, which will create success in the future. There will always be surprises and new hazards along the way as well as opportunities. It emphasizes the need for marketing to be creative. Watch this space. The next edition of this book will probably consist of a disc the size of a penny that will slot into a personal player, and read itself out to you in the voice of your choice while projecting the words and pictures on the ceiling as you lie in the bath.

If you are new to marketing all this and more will be what provides the challenges for the future. Of one prediction we can be sure, at least some of the challenges will be unexpected and many will demand different ideas and solutions from those that have worked in the past.

> If you are not bloodying your nose in today's warp-speed economy, we have a name for you. Dead.
>
> *Forbes ASAP*

As the saying has it: *the future isn't what it used to be.* That being so, how will you get on? It is to that we turn next.

My interest is in the future because I am going to spend the rest of my life there.

Charles F Kettering

The future has a way of arriving unannounced.

George F Will

8

Will you make a successful marketer?

The trouble with being in the fast lane is that you get to the other end in an awful hurry.

John Jensen

So there you are, you should now understand the full cycle of marketing, from a philosophy of customer orientation through a range of activities from research to after-sales service. There really is much more to it than just advertisement or selling. It encompasses a whole function of business, and, in a company which grows into a multinational, literally the whole world. Marketing, as we have seen, is a complex process. Any commercial success it may produce has as much to do with the orchestration of its many techniques as individual excellence in one of them. What is really key? It may help to summarize around what I refer to as the five 'C's.

1. Marketing's first 'C' is the **customer.** The focus of the entire marketing effort is external. The customer is truly King (or Queen) and without customers buying and buying again there

is no profit. Any company that forgets this for even a tiny instant is likely to be in big trouble.

2. The second is **continuous**. Marketing is not an option, a 'bolt-on' activity for when time allows. Marketing must drive the business continuously, and without it there is no progress.

3. Next, **co-ordinated**; the marketer is the arch puppeteer. Every-thing reviewed here must be made to interrelate operationally. It is no good, for instance, having an advertising campaign that has potential customers rushing to the shops only to find that the product is nowhere in evidence because distribution is lagging behind. This does not just lose sales, it does permanent damage. So the marketer needs to keep pulling all the strings together.

4. Fourth comes **creative.** Marketing must continuously seek for new ways to maintain awareness and differentiate from comp-etition. This is not just a question of creative ideas. It probably *seemed* a good idea for Hoover to offer free flights to America, but the promotion was ill conceived and did more harm than good. Creative ideas must be appropriate to their task; and they must work.

5. Last, but by no means least, **culture.** One marketing person, or even a whole marketing department cannot do the whole job by themselves. Many people, throughout the organization, act to ensure ultimate success. So, if the marketers want the credit for success in the market place, they must *create* a marketing culture that supports and plays its part in all that makes marketing work.

It is a considerable, and by no means easy, task to make marketing successful. It is, or should be, the driving force behind industry and those in marketing see themselves as out in front, at the sharp end. Is it for you?

OVERHEARD

In my company the marketing director is so senior he has people to delegate *for* him.

By definition the marketer in any company is in a senior management role. It is a position which demands experience, real experience over some years not one year's experience multiplied by 5 or 10; and real expertise. Sounds like you already? The marketer needs to work first in one of the many different areas of marketing, he may start in sales or research, or he may become a brand, or product, manager responsible for one brand – a sort of mini-marketing manager. The best background will give him a broad understanding of all the marketing techniques and detailed knowledge where necessary; he must be a jack of all trades and master of some. Marketing demands a strategic view (where are we going?). It demands a scientific approach, that starts by identifying opportunities; collects, sorts and analyses data; formulates solutions; tests; implements and does so relentlessly as market conditions change. In addition the marketer must be a good manager, able to make sure the team all play their part.

And they must be numerate, have commercial awareness and flair, understand any technology their area of marketing may involve and be open-minded and creative. Marketing may, in part, be about applying tried and tested methodology, but it is also an ideas business and the ability to innovate must come high on the list of criteria for success. Still sound like you?

A rewarding challenge

Certainly, marketing is rarely easy.

It is a challenging role. Markets are fickle and unforgiving. Opportunities are all too often disguised as hard work. Solutions must be implemented creatively. Synergy may be an important element. Synergy is the process by which 2 plus 2 makes 5. A good trick if you can do it. In fact it is what creative management is all about.

Marketing is art and science inextricably blended. It abounds with theory and the literature available on it is as wide as in any area of management, wider than in many. There is a new magic formula, a new guru every five minutes. Gurus, incidentally, are simply marketers who have chosen to market a product very dear to them: themselves. However, before you decide to become a marketing guru remember what was said about the product life cycle.

No individual theory guarantees success in marketing. Nor has success got anything to do with good luck, though this on the other hand is no doubt the prime reason for your competitors' success.

> It is what you learn after you know it all that counts.
>
> John Wooden

The marketer walks the tightrope between startling success and utter failure. What matters in marketing? Profits. The successful marketer is the one who brings home the bacon, whose company prospers. Ultimately none of the other measures like market share, the percentage of the available market a product has, matters. All that does matter is profitability, and this can stem only from satisfied customers. Marketers are not judged by activity, rather by achievement.

If you become involved in marketing you will be judged, and paid, on results. It is not the kind of kitchen to get into if you do not like the heat. For those who succeed it provides a rewarding, satisfying and worthwhile career; marketing promotes trade, industry and employment. You really will be keeping the wheels of industry turning.

Besides, however uncertain, however much it is hard work, marketing is fun; and that is even more important.

The only place where success comes before work is in the dictionary.

Vidal Sassoon

Glossary

The following list, while making no attempt to be comprehensive, is designed to act as a quick reference to key marketing terms. By its very nature jargon in any field changes as you watch (after all it is not so impressive to use a term *everyone* understands). The successful marketer will keep up to date with the prevailing jargon; and, when desperate measures are necessary, invent their own.

> Somebody else's ignorance is bliss.
>
> Jack Vance

Advertising the umbrella term for all persuasive messages in 'bought space', incorporating media from TV and newspapers to bus tickets and litter bins.

Advertising budget a bottomless pit.

Benchmarking in marketing: this implies comparison with competitors in such areas as quality or service.

Brand extension using the same brand name across a widening range of, perhaps rather different, products.

Brand positioning accurately relating one brand to its competitors in terms of price, quality and appeal.

Brand strategy the method chosen to successfully achieve the objectives set for marketing the brand.

Channels of distribution the 'routes' along which it is decided to send a product to market; such routes *are* variable though many companies regard them as fixed – for example, who would have guessed a few years ago we would buy pizza and bulk quantities of potatoes from petrol filling stations?

Churning the launch of a whole range of slightly different products with the realistic aim of making only some of them succeed (as is done, for instance, with holidays).

'Clevver marketting' a term used, in writing, to describe marketing communications and branding that plays fast and loose with correct spelling: an example is the motor car the Mazda Millenia.

Commission bribes to get salespeople, agents and others to do their job.

Competition the enemy, of which you should take a broad view when defining, and which you should never take your eye off for one second.

Copy pollution a term applied from the customers' perspective that describes a certain, actually unhelpful, over-the-top description of something offered. An example is the pretentious menu describing basic dishes as if they are something unusually wonderful.

Customer otherwise the client, prospect or punter; the focus of all marketing attention – no customers, no marketing job.

Customer care the umbrella term for everything to do with customer service; can – well handled – be a major factor in differentiating you from competition, but is inherently fragile and failure to meet customer expectations can quickly lose sales.

Customer relationship management (CMR) the systematic, and often computer-system-assisted, process of creating, maintaining and developing business relationships with customers, especially major ones.

Database marketing marketing using sophisticated analysis of computerized customer and prospect lists to direct marketing action accurately (so when I am mailed as Ms Forsithe, there is really no excuse).

Direct mail a first class way of selling; promotion by post, don't we all love it!

Direct response advertising (or direct mail) that depends on individual direct response; clipping, completing and returning a coupon, for example.

E-commerce the umbrella term for the whole process of doing business on the Internet.

Integrated marketing (or communication) the concept of ensuring that marketing is integrated into the other functions and activities of the organization; an entirely sensible approach and, perhaps sadly, likely to be more effective than marketing located in an ivory tower and doing everything in isolation.

Loyalty schemes schemes, often involving issuing loyalty cards, that encourage repeat purchase and customer loyalty. They range from frequent flyer schemes with airlines to cards that link the customer to a retail group or supermarket chain. They are used not least for the information that their use produces. This creates a powerful database, which in turn allows more precise promotional activity to be deployed.

Market map a device for tracking the variety of routes to market and the different kinds of customer potentially involved.

Market research the process of attempting to find out what increasingly fickle customers want.

Market segment a homogeneous group of customers who have similar characteristics or who respond in similar ways. A segment must be numerous enough to be worthwhile targeting and accessible – communication and supply of product must be able to be directed at them.

Marketing concept the core maxim of marketing: business can only be successful through appropriate customer focus.

Marketing culture the orchestration of everyone in the company in a way that ensures that their different roles truly support the customer focus; and persuading them that doing so is necessary.

Marketing objectives the results (financial, share of market etc) that it is decided to target.

Marketing planning the analysis and decision that sets out what marketing activity will be implemented, how, when, where and by whom.

Marketing research this is research that is designed to investigate marketing methods, with an eye on improving how they work. It includes attempts to ascertain the effectiveness of advertising, but can be applied to any detail of marketing activity.

Marketing strategy the method selected to achieve the results targeted; the 'route' taken.

Marketing tactics the nitty gritty of day-to-day action that fine-tunes the strategy and responds to market circumstances.

Media planning the complex and perhaps uncertain process of choosing where advertising is placed amongst the plethora of media options available in order to get the best results.

Mission statement an Americanism which may nevertheless be helpful to clarify corporate intention: it is a succinct statement of organization values and intentions designed to focus thinking and aid communication and common purposes.

Negotiation starts where selling leaves off, and may make the difference between profitability or being taken to the cleaners.

New product launch a risky business not to be undertaken lightly.

Niche marketing activity focused on very precise segments – the opposite of all things to all people.

Partnership marketing implies that more than one organization is involved. There is a collaboration of some sort between two or more organizations usually to maximize marketing effectiveness and often to reduce costs. An airline and a hotel group might work together in this way and the logical relationship between them in the eyes of customers makes such collaboration possible.

Permission marketing the tactic and communication of getting a customer to allow you to contact them regularly by e-mail or by personalizing what they see when they log onto a Web site.

Pester-power the influence brought on parents by young children to buy them things; marketing aims to create such pressure in the way it communicates with children and to create acceptance of it in the way it communicates with parents. Causes some controversy – where should the line be drawn?

Pricing theory an uncertain body of knowledge, not to be relied on in isolation.

Product life cycle the stages over time that a product goes through, from product launch through growth and on to demise or deletion. Marketing activity must vary in light of the stage of the life cycle that a product is at, and depending on how it is intended to influence its progress. Long life cycles are preferable to short, if only so that the marketer responsible is long gone by the time product senility sets in.

Profit what, in most organizations, marketing is about generating; ultimately, unless the shareholders or owners are financially happy there may be troubles ahead.

Promotional mix the phrase used to describe the range of promotional options that exist and highlight the fact that they must be made to work together, not used in isolation.

Public relations all those areas of publicity that help create the right image of, and opinion about, an organization; often abbreviated to PR and also used to mean press relations which is only part of overall public relations.

Re-branding changing the name, and often also the image of a product to give it a new look or to reposition it; the product specification itself may or may not change.

Relationship marketing consists of planned, systematic communication to keep in touch and develop on-going and increasing business from existing customers; a sort of long-term corporate chat-up.

Sales forecasting the process of anticipating the inevitable and then taking the credit for it.

Sales promotion the plethora of publicity devices that are part of the overall marketing effort, from price reduction to competition, sponsorship and events.

Segmentation recognizing that markets consist of sub-sections with specific and different needs, identifying and focusing as appropriate to win business.

Selling personal, one to one, persuasive communication whether done by sales people or others and whether done face-to-face or, say, on the telephone.

Social Marketing this term refers to marketing activity carried out by non-profit making organizations, or rather those which intentionally aim not to make profit. Most often it is applied to those organizations that do something worthwhile, such as charities, fund raising and campaigning bodies – even government (in regard to campaigns to reduce drink driving, for instance). There are those who would regard some publishers and authors as being in this category!

SWOT initials standing for: strengths and weaknesses, opportunities and threats; characterizes an approach to the analysis demanded in effective planning.

USP initials standing for unique selling proposition; essentially what it is about a product or service that makes people likely to buy it in preference to other competing offerings – if you do not have any start worrying now.

Web site not quite the gold at the end of the rainbow, but the latest, technologically based marketing method – the advertisement, catalogue or source of information about an organization or product that someone can dial into via the Internet. Increasingly this provides a facility for direct ordering (using a credit card). Large amounts of business are being conducted this way from purchase of books and CDs to interactive auctions of property. (You can click on *amazon.co.uk* to order more copies of this book and hardly lift your eyes from the page as you do so. Try it!). A fascinating development, and one where there is every sign of its still being in its infancy.

Appendix: how high can you go?

A checklist to show whether you are a potential marketing director

As has already been said, the marketer needs to be a jack of all trades and a master of some. Specifically the top marketer will need:

- knowledge of the major marketing methods and techniques (10 years' rounded experience or a quick scan of this book should suffice)

- to be an *effective manager* (ie, be able to recruit, select, train, plan, organize and control a diverse team of creative and often difficult people)

- to take the *long view* (ie, direct the business, set strategic objectives and define a framework of targets, priorities and policies to drive towards them)

- to understand and be able to work with the *other business functions* (yes, even the financial director)

- to be *numerate* (if only so you know when to take a bow or leave the sinking ship)

- to understand and be able to work with those aspects of *the new technology* that are necessary within your area of marketing (and to hold your own with the geeks you must work with in IT)

- to be *productive*, use time effectively and focus on the key issues (do you complete the marketing plan or play golf with the managing director?)

- to make *effective decisions* (at least as often as, and preferably more often than, your colleagues)

- to *communicate effectively* (and that means persuading not telling people what to do)

- to *stay close to the market*, really to understand the customers (even to the point of talking to some of them, or even using the product yourself)

- to *achieve results*, not just organize activities (there are no gold stars in marketing just for being busy)

How High Can You Go?
Tick how you rate yourself

	1	2	3	4	5	6
	Excellent – I can write a book on it	No problem	Will be all right on the night	Well, maybe	Frankly, needs working on	Do not even think it is necessary

Rate yourself on the scale from 1–6. If there are too many 5s and 6s consider some less challenging occupation, like brain surgery or nuclear physics. If you rate yourself consistently 2, drop me a line – you will need to be seen to be believed; consistently 1, drop the publisher a line – they are used to dealing with prima donnas. Finally, if you are a marketing director and rate 6s, you should perhaps buy shares in your main competitor.

POSTSCRIPT

It is said that if a man goes to a party and says to a woman that she needs a man and should come home with him; that's marketing. If he stands on a chair and declares to the assembled company his expertise and availability in matters of love; that is advertising. If he tells the woman he is the world's greatest lover and that she should come home with him at once; that's selling. And if she comes to him and says she hears he is the world's greatest lover, will he please come home with her; that's public relations. And a good trick for those who can do it.

ERRATUM

This slip has been inserted by mistake.

Alisdair Gray

Other books written by Patrick Forsyth and published by Kogan Page include:

Marketing Professional Services
Marketing on a Tight Budget
101 Ways to Increase Your Sales
Powerful Reports and Proposals
How to Get a Top Job in Marketing
How to Get a Top Job in Sales and Business Development
Developing Your Staff
How to Motivate People

Also five titles in the mini-book series *30 Minutes*:

30 Minutes Before a Presentation
30 Minutes to Write a Report
30 Minutes to Motivate Your Staff
30 Minutes Before Your Appraisal
30 Minutes to Get Your Own Way

The above titles are available from all good bookshops. For further information, please contact the publisher at the following address:

Kogan Page Limited
120 Pentonville Road
London N1 9JN
Tel: 020 7278 0433
Fax: 020 7837 6348
www.kogan-page.co.uk